THE COMPLETE BOOK OF HOUSEPLANTS UNDER LIGHTS

THE COMPLETE BOOK
OF HOUSEPLANTS
UNDER LIGHTS
by CHARLES MARDEN FITCH

Photographs by the author unless otherwise credited

A Helen Van Pelt Wilson Book

HAWTHORN BOOKS, INC.
PUBLISHERS/New York

THE COMPLETE BOOK OF HOUSEPLANTS UNDER LIGHTS

Library of Congress Catalog Card Number: 75-5041.
ISBN: 0-8015-1496-7
1 2 3 4 5 6 7 8 9 10

For my friends throughout the developing countries of tropical Africa, Asia, and Latin America; may time, technology, and temperament permit us to protect nature's beauty while we work for improved lives in our varied cultures.

Contents

Acknowledgments   ix

PART I

Basics of Light Gardening

1 Gardens Under Lights   3
2 Light in Nature   12
3 Fixtures for Light Gardens   19
4 Custom-Designed Light Gardens   32
5 The Quality of Light   46
6 Night Into Day   68
7 The Environment: Air, Humidity, Temperature   76
8 Containers and Methods of Watering   85
9 Potting Mixes and Fertilizers   99

vii

PART II

Plants to Grow

10	*Gesneriads, Champions Under Lights*	113
11	*Orchids All Year Long*	128
12	*Geraniums for Bloom and Scent*	153
13	*A Gourmet's Garden of Herbs*	159
14	*A Foliage Rainbow*	163
15	*Begonias for Flowers and Foliage*	180
16	*Cacti and Other Succulents*	193
17	*International Flowers—Tender and Hardy Bulbs*	209
18	*Bromeliads, the Durable Air Plants*	222
19	*Propagation—Increasing Beauty Under Lights*	229
20	*If Pests or Disease Strike*	239
21	*Plant Societies and Sources of Equipment*	248
	Bibliography	259
	Index	261

Acknowledgments

A complete reference book such as this involves an extraordinary amount of testing and research. This exacting but pleasant work has been made easier by many friends who shared their horticultural findings and by research personnel in several areas.

Among those who deserve special mention for their friendly cooperation are Dr. Henry M. Cathey, chief of the Ornamentals Laboratory of the United States Department of Agriculture station in Beltsville, Maryland; Helen Van Pelt Wilson, patient editor and experienced gardener; Christopher Quinn, my imaginative photographic assistant; Dr. George Kalmbacher, taxonomist with the Brooklyn Botanic Garden; Jack Golding, President of the Indoor Light Gardening Society; and many members of the tropical plant societies listed in Chapter 21.

We should all express gratitude to the commercial growers and hybridizers who year after year offer home gardeners the best in ornamental cultivars, thereby increasing our pleasure in growing houseplants under lights.

PART I

BASICS OF
LIGHT GARDENING

1

Gardens Under Lights

You need light for living, and this same illumination around your home can help you grow beautiful houseplants. You can create gardens all over your house, double the growing space in a greenhouse, or turn your basement into a tropical paradise by gardening under lights. Dim hallways, spare rooms, closets, bookshelves, and heated garages offer other possibilities. Contemplating delicate flowers or exquisite foliage can be a healthy tranquilizer, like the enjoyment of relaxing music. In the middle of the coldest winters, you can enjoy fragrant orchids and warm terrariums thriving under fluorescent lights.

Lights for Indoor Plants

When indoor gardeners began growing houseplants under fluorescent lights, it was the custom to compile long lists of those species which "grew under fluorescents." After more than twenty years of experimenting with countless species in numerous genera, I find it more practical to recommend certain light intensities or to note how various species perform under different types of tubes. I have yet to find a houseplant

An indoor greenhouse where fluorescents provide fourteen hours of bright light each day has turned this basement into a year-round garden.

that *does not* grow under fluorescent lamps and, in most cases, thrive to the point of blooming or producing abundant, attractive foliage.

Some plants do best with modern horticultural fluorescent tubes (see Chapter 5); others grow satisfactorily with standard household lights, such as Cool Whites. Excellent blooming results with a wide range of plants when sunlight is supplemented by fluorescent lamps. In this book I feature the best available varieties in each genus, including numerous new hybrids, all selected for their attractiveness when grown indoors under artificial light where plants know only sunny days.

To Help the Sun

Fluorescent lights and even incandescent bulbs are useful in the home and greenhouse to supplement sunlight. The best results under my conditions have been with fluorescent lamps specifically formulated to provide the *kind* of light most utilized by green plants.

Whenever possible, locate your light gardens where they can also receive some daylight. This saves energy and produces the best flowering. Some daylight is especially important if you use standard Cool or Warm White household fluorescents instead of horticultural lamps.

Several lighting companies produce fluorescent tubes specifically designed for growing plants. The first to achieve national acceptance was Sylvania's Gro-Lux. This rosy-hued light turns plain colors into glowing phosphorescent tones. Colored foliage, like that of the creeping *Zebrina*, *Coleus blumei*, or *Cissus discolor*, turns into a psychedelic wonder

An incandescent floodlight provides supplemental energy for this plant while creating a dramatic nighttime picture.

under standard Gro-Lux light. Other developments in horticultural lamps are covered fully in Chapter 5.

Multipurpose Lights

It is ecologically and financially wise to conserve electrical energy. This serving is easily accomplished by using lights to serve several simultaneous functions. In dark halls arrange fluorescents to illuminate the passage while also providing adequate intensity for low-light requirement ferns, philodendrons, or creeping *Ficus*. Beauty and safety can be served by one switch. A similar dual function results when a desk or reading lamp provides supplemental illumination for foliage plants while it serves to light your work.

A school, in which I work as media specialist, is quite new and, although it was costly to build, the architects neglected to provide light in the foyer of our television studio. Since the area has no windows and no wall light switch, it was very dim. We solved this problem by installing a light stand with two tiers of plant trays, illuminated by aluminum fixtures holding two 40-watt lamps each.

Filling the trays with white perlite (volcanic rock) gives bottom reflection, and pushing the stand against a white wall reflects light from behind onto foliage and into the foyer. An automatic timer turns on the lamps in the morning and shuts them off at night for an average 14-hour day, except through long vacations. Then we cut down light-hours to ten thus reducing the amount of water required by the plants.

Installing the light stand has:

1. Provided light in an otherwise dangerously dark foyer.
2. Produced an attractive vista of living beauty in a windowless studio.
3. Introduced numerous students and teachers to exotic tropical plants.

This stainless steel and wood light garden forms an unusual room divider. A translucent top gives diffuse room lighting and illuminates a crystal collection. Light fixtures can contain two, three, or four 40-watt lamps. (General Electric photo)

Some students take home cuttings or divisions. They are thus gently introduced to a rewarding avocation that will complement their lives no matter what they study or become.

Basement Beauty

Even a single fluorescent in a dull basement can furnish enough light to grow ferns, bright *Zebrinas*, and African-violets. Under a fixture with two 40-watt tubes your gardening possibilities are greatly increased, and you are only a step away from filling the basement with flowers! I write this with

Vertical lamps at both sides, hidden by an ornamental frame, furnish adequate light for a trailing *Columnea*. An additional tube overhead would make an even better situation for sturdy growth.

pleasure but also as a warning. When it is so easy to provide good growing conditions anywhere, the engaging result for most light gardeners is expansion. Today the basement, tomorrow the hall closet, next year a living-room wall all overflowing with exotic plants under lights.

Where Else?

Light used to be the most difficult environmental requirement for plants indoors. Unless you were blessed with sunny windows, it was impossible to have flowering plants all year long. Without adequate light even holiday gift plants quickly faded. Now with inexpensive fluorescent lighting you can create artificial sun anywhere, or supplement the sunlight already reaching your plants. Sun combined with fluorescent light is one way to turn even dull rooms and north windows into plant showcases.

Potted plants that have developed handsomely with fluorescent lights in out-of-the-way places are prime candidates for upward mobility. Move them around for your enjoyment. Although areas of a living room or bedroom may have insufficient light to grow sturdy plants, you can safely keep light-garden specimens in these dim places for a week or two.

Portability of plants gives you freedom to grow perfect specimens anywhere and to display them wherever you wish. With supplemental light from reading lamps or overhead reflector bulbs your portable specimens will last even longer in decorative splendor. After ten to fifteen days, move them back under fluorescents where sturdy growth can develop for a future showing.

Props At Hand

Holiday gift plants or other houseplants grown for special occasions can be kept in good condition under portable fluorescent fixtures. In a cool Bogota television studio, nearly 9,000 feet in the Colombian Andes, I used fluorescent lamps to maintain healthy plants originally grown in tropical sunshine. We were recording a series of programs dealing with biology in which I wanted to show living specimens rather than drawings or photographs of plants. The problem was that we could only videotape two or three programs per day, every other day of the week. Then various tropical plants presented in the series would be used again in a final review, weeks away on the studio recording calendar.

Recalling my previous experience with orchids and bromeliads in New York, I had the studio electrician install a fluorescent fixture behind our science set in the dark studio.

After each program the prop plants were transferred from the program table to our indoor sunshine. Although the tubes were only standard Cool Whites they kept our living examples in excellent condition for over a month.

You can do the same thing to maintain holiday gift plants or sturdy cuttings you have potted for your friends. Well-made, freestanding fixtures are available from a number of mail-order firms (see Chapter 21), and at some local garden centers. It takes only a few minutes to set up one of these portable fixtures. With little effort and about eighteen dollars you can prepare a fine growing-place with enough room for several plants under two 20-watt lamps, ready to keep *your* props in full splendor for many a day.

Temperatures

Since you can furnish light so easily, the other environmental factors set the only limit for indoor plants. Temperature is perhaps the most critical since humidity, as I show in Chapter

This young student's room reflects a rewarding interest in nature, with something new to discover every day. A bottle garden doubles as a lamp base, and the bookshelf garden provides light for adaptable succulents set close to 20-watt tubes.

EVEREST
THE WEST RIDGE

MASSACHUS

Discover Wildlife

7, can be maintained with just a little planning. The temperature in living areas is suitable for almost all the tropicals you will want to grow. Gesneriads, especially African-violets, most begonias, thousands of orchids, the majority of bromeliads, and countless foliage plants are all satisfied with the 65°–70° minimum nights we maintain in living quarters. If you let nights drop into the low 60s to save fuel, the plants will be just as happy.

When you want cooler- or warmer-than-average temperatures for certain species, microclimates can be formed under lights (see Chapter 7). So begin thinking about your indoor garden paradise. Plan to brighten the basement, liven up the living room, cast light on a dim corner. Perhaps my photographs will give you some ideas.

2
Light in Nature

In nature green plants are exposed to the full spectrum of sunlight. You have seen the beautiful bands of rainbow hues transformed to basic colors when the sun shines through a prism or through water vapor. Sunlight is what sustains green plants and all other life, for it is earth's original energy source, the key to the conversion of light into organic materials through photosynthesis, the process by which plants manufacture food within green leaves.

Brightness

In any given portion of sky, sunlight has an even brilliance, corresponding to the season, but by the time sunlight reaches green plants on earth it has been modified in several ways. First the atmosphere—including water vapor, suspended solid particles, and gases—filters sunlight. Some ultraviolet rays, harmful to life, are not let through this atmospheric curtain. Second, once sunlight reaches our life zone or biosphere, the clouds, including tropical mists and coastal fogs, further reduce light intensity.

In regions where rainfall is sufficient for tall trees, plants adapted to full sun grow tall, providing shade for other species below. (In jungles and tropical woods I often find four or five different light zones.) Plants evolve to survive in a *precise* range of sunlight. Of course, soil moisture, humidity, and temperature interact with light intensity to form the ideal habitat for each species. In captivity these interrelating factors determine the growth of our houseplants.

We might deduce that plants are thus confined to a precise microclimate and that any variation would cause death. Fortunately this is not the case for most ornamental tropicals. Very few species have such specialized requirements that they cannot accept some deviation from the conditions of their habitats. Furthermore, by crossing different species and creating hybrids among genera, plant breeders have further increased the adaptability of ornamental houseplants. Thus, although certain basic environmental characteristics may be

In the mountains of New Zealand I found ferns and evergreens which required a moist, cool habitat with bright, diffuse light. Even in the tropics, orchids, such as *Odtontoglossums*, thrive in similar conditions on high mountain slopes. Cool-growing houseplants from high altitudes or the semitropics are easier to grow under fluorescents than in sunlight.

present in their natural habitats, you can successfully grow the same sort of plants under slightly different conditions.

Even so do not expect a sun-adapted cactus to make healthy growth in dim light, or an *Episcia* from the jungle floor to thrive in intense light or low humidity. It is an advantage for us that fluorescent light is easier to manage than sunshine. Houseplants that would normally burn under the sun's direct rays will accept bright fluorescent light because there is less heat and no window glass magnifies solar rays.

Sun and Shade

Scientific observations made in various tropical regions indicate that plants on the forest floor often receive less than one quarter of the sunlight that falls on treetops above. For example, in Malayan jungles the tall trees are in full sun, while shade plants living in ground-level humus get only 1/100th as much light. In South America, New Guinea, and East Africa I found sun-loving orchids high in the trees, while shade-tolerant species grew in lower crotches or on understory shrubs.

Cacti, adapted to thrive in strong sun, often grow several feet tall like this *Opuntia* in Yucatan. Small propagations, seedlings, or naturally dwarf species are best for light gardens.

14

Light is strong, nights rather chilly over much of East Africa. Animals can wander in search of water, but plants must conserve what little moisture they receive by their waxy coverings, succulent parts, or by dropping some leaves. This is a section of Serengeti, Tanzania.

These variations work to our advantage in light gardening. Epiphytic *Cattleya* orchids, which normally perch in high branches, thrive under the center of fluorescent lamps where light is most intense. Toward the fixture ends, where intensity drops off, we can place ladyslipper orchids (*Paphiopedilum*) which grow on the ground in nature. Next to them, toward the ends and edges, ferns, trailing philodendrons, and similar low-light requirement species will thrive.

Light Color, Top to Bottom

It might seem reasonable that sunlight is sunlight, with standard variations according to the time of day. We all know that sunrises and sunsets have a warmer color than noontime sun, but research shows that even during the day sunlight has different colors, depending on where it falls.

For example, at the tops of trees, high in the branches where many orchids and bromeliads live, or in the desert where there

Forest-floor species and epiphytic orchids, adapted to live in shade from overhead branches, die of sunburn in a day or two when jungle trees are removed for road-building in this Amazon region of Brazil and Colombia.

are no overhead leaves, the sun's rays have a high concentration of red and far-red radiation. In the jungle or forest, where rays travel through foliage to reach plants below, they have much more of the violet–blue tones. Thus *Marantas* and *Episcias* normally receive less red and far-red light than orchids or bromeliads in the treetops.

This confirms the results of the tests I have made with fluorescent lamps that have different spectrums. The GTE Sylvania Company also recommends that plants with full-sun requirements be grown under their Wide Spectrum Gro-Lux lamps rather than under the standard violet–blue-toned Gro-Lux. In practice, species that come from regions of high-light intensity and are adapted to almost full sun will do best under wide-spectrum lamps. Forest-floor tropicals, which include most foliage plants and many gesneriads, do perfectly well under the standard Gro-Lux lamps or combinations of Daylight, Cool White, or natural household fluorescents.

Dawn to Dusk

Around the equator the tropical sun rises and sets at about the same time throughout the year. Since dark and light periods are almost equal there, plants usually receive their cues for growth changes from variations in moisture or temperature rather than from night- or day-length. This is not true for species from semitropical regions where variations in night-length are greater with seasonal changes.

Under lights in captivity some species grow better when we give them longer days. Other species may grow well but fail to flower if nights are shorter than 12 hours. Fortunately, most houseplants thrive with a 12- to 18-hour day-range, regardless

Humans see best with light in the yellow-green part of the spectrum, but research indicates that green plants are most sensitive to blue and orange-red light (labeled in nanometers). Colors of the spectrum, shown along the top left to right, are violet, blue, green, yellow, orange, red. Actually colors change and blend gradually, as seen in a rainbow. (Diagram based on information from GTE Sylvania)

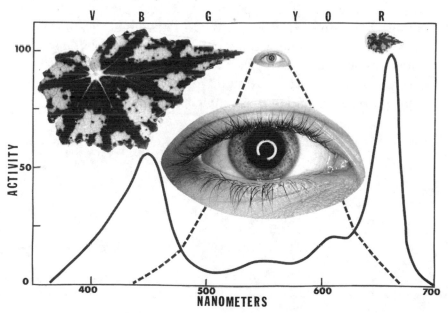

of what nature provides for them in the tropics. (Day-length is considered in detail in Chapter 6.)

Secrets Revealed

It is interesting that money spent to learn about growth patterns of health-inhibiting *Nicotiana tabacum* has resulted in findings that also enrich our lives with beauty and peace. The thousands of federal tax dollars spent on tobacco studies by the United States Department of Agriculture have produced useful information regarding the influence of light on all green plants. Day-length responses discovered in these early experiments have formed a basis for the creation of the horticultural fluorescent lamps, tubes with tailored spectrums that illuminate houseplants in homes from coast to coast today. Thousands of gardeners now have a healthy addiction to growing plants indoors.

Pioneer experiments in plant reactions to day-length, the research of many universities, and continuing studies by the U.S.D.A. have thus produced practical findings applicable to indoor gardening. However, to read through the original research would not only require a great deal of time but also an in-depth scientific knowledge that few home gardeners possess. On that account, I have outlined the findings, applied them to indoor gardening, and incorporated them in this book.

3
Fixtures for Light Gardens

Standard fluorescent fixtures, to be found in almost every hardware store, are suitable even for custom-designed light gardens, such as room dividers or areas illuminated for plants. The advantages of using these common fixtures are their availability and low price. Where space above plants is limited, as in cabinets or bookshelves, install slim, reflectorless fixtures, but paint adjacent surfaces flat white or provide mirrors to increase reflection and so double the view of your plants.

Reflectors

Use reflector fixtures over basement plant tables, under greenhouse benches, and in other places where four to six inches can be spared for a reflector. Baked white enamel and polished aluminum reflectors are both suitable. Aluminum reflectors are lightweight and bright, but after a year or so they need scrubbing with a cleanser to get rid of the dulling film that forms. If you paint aluminum reflectors with flat white metal paint, you need only wipe them off occasionally.

Baked enamel reflectors are standard with most fixtures; the white surface is excellent but the metal construction is heavy.

Miniature 8-watt tube suitable for terrarium supplemental light or other uses where space is limited.

Some popular plant stands and tiered carts, such as the Flora Cart (Tube Craft Co.), come with white steel reflectors. Fixtures from the Shoplite Company feature all-aluminum construction.

The simplest way to provide light over plants is to buy fixtures constructed for light gardening. They are usually supplied with convenient switches, efficient reflectors, and some provision for hanging. Legs to permit fixtures to stand free are available from some manufacturers.

Table Fixtures

When you don't want to hang or permanently install a fixture, purchase one of the self-supporting units designed to stand on legs above a plant tray. Typical of this design is Sylvania's Gro-Lamp and the portable Combolite of Tube Craft. Waterproof trays of plastic, fiberglass, or aluminum to fit neatly under these light fixtures are offered by various suppliers.

Some companies, such as Shoplite, offer tabletop kits complete with waterproof tray and freestanding fluorescent fixture suitable for placement on a table or other flat surface. If you don't find the color tray or fixture that complements your decor, simply cover the exterior of reflector and tray with some color paint. But keep the inside of a reflector white and do not paint the polished aluminum part.

Circline Fixtures

The round table lamps designed for plants are fitted with circline tubes. Most of these are supplied with efficient Wide-Spectrum Gro-Lux lamps, excellent for African-violets and similar tropicals. The one drawback to the circline units currently offered is that the push-in light switches will not work automatically on timers. You have to turn the units *on* manually, but a timer *can* turn them off.

Nevertheless, I do recommend desktop circline fixtures as practical and attractive. They are well suited to offices, since lovely flowering and foliage plants can be kept growing with little space or care required. Fill the tray with moist gravel or perlite to provide humidity. Leave the light on from morning to late afternoon, but not for 24 hours a day.

Vita-Lite lamps fit in standard fluorescent fixtures. The Power-Twist version gives about 10 percent more light than the plain tube.

This Shoplite aluminum and redwood light garden features bright aluminum reflectors and four tiers of growing space.

Tiered Stands

Professionally built stands with two or more levels for plants often make the most efficient light gardens, especially where you wish to grow many plants in a limited space. I concentrate on the plants rather than the structure of a stand so I think well-designed plant stands are suitable for living areas in your home. By placing trailing foliage and some ferns toward the front and both sides of each tier, you can conceal much of the frame, softening the lines considerably.

To customize a commercial light stand just paint the frame and fixture tops with your choice of color. Rust-Oleum and similar metal paints work well on reflector tops. Aerosol cans make even painting easy, but spraying should be done outside or in a very well ventilated room away from plants. Brush application is best where you must paint near furniture. Permit all parts to dry several days before placing plants on the stand.

An easy-to-assemble circline table lamp provides adequate light for African-violets, begonias, and similar species.

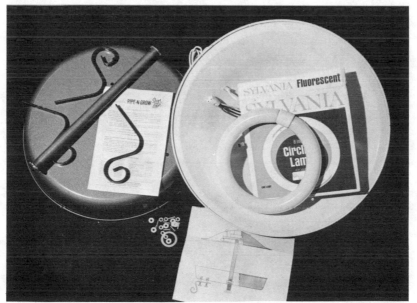

Designs

Nationally available light stands include a redwood unit with aluminum corner posts (Shoplite Co.), the tubular aluminum Flora Cart (Tube Craft Co.), an all-steel gold-tube frame with styrene trays and enameled steel reflector (The Green House), galvanized steel and aluminum Hobby House stands (Geo. W. Park Seed Co.), and a lightweight aluminum tube Lumen-liter stand (Floralite Co.). All of these fixtures are offered by the mail-order firms listed in Chapter 21. Sizes vary from two-level 20-watt stands to four-tier units with fixtures holding four 40-watt lamps each.

Decorator Hobby House light stand by the Park Seed Company has two lighted shelves. (Geo. W. Park Co. photo)

For efficient operation, fixtures usually have an accessory plug input so two or more units can be plugged together. The terminal light fixture is then plugged into the timer connected to an electric outlet. All fixtures then go on and off simultaneously, according to how you program the timer dial. (14-16 hours are suitable for most houseplants. Details are given in Chapter 6.)

Indoor Garden Cabinets

Several glass cabinets designed for growing indoor plants incorporate light fixtures. The Phytarium is an elaborate and expensive sophisticated growth chamber supplied with controls for heat, humidity, ventilation, and light. An optional accessory lets you add carbon dioxide for more rapid growth. Somewhat similar is the Phyto-Gro chamber of Aladdin Industries.

This decorator-styled metal stand holds two 20-watt lamps per shelf. It is suitable for display or for growing medium-light requirement plants. (Fleco Industries photo)

The Phyto-Gro chamber permits you to control ventilation, light, and humidity. Basic construction is fiberglass with clear plastic doors. Timer at the top controls the on/off periods of the lights. (Aladdin Industries Inc. photo)

Less complicated are the glass cases offered by Lord & Burnham as the Solar Plantariums. These permit control of ventilation and temperature with sliding glass doors and hinged tops. A deluxe Plantarium (48 inches long, 22 inches high) can be ordered with a fixture for 40-watt lamps; the Mini Plantarium (25½ inches long, 20 inches high) is available with a 20-watt Gro-Lite.

Similar cases are occasionally offered in mail-order catalogs. Prices range from about $50.00 to more than $200.00, but these professionally built chambers are more useful and attractive

The Solar Plantarium protects houseplants by conserving humidity. Two 40-watt fluorescents give enough light for many species; the inside pan is filled with moist gravel. (Lord and Burnham Co. photo)

This heavy-duty timer controls several fixtures.

than improvised arrangements for preserving humidity. For example, a plastic tent, a tray with moist gravel, and a free-standing lamp are practical but hardly as pleasing in an office or living room as a tastefully constructed garden cabinet or Wardian case with fluorescent lighting.

Glarefree Lights

Modern wedged louvers (Para-Wedge and Paracube) of polystyrene coated with silver or gold and plain white plastic acrylic louvers cut off brightness at a 45° angle. When the louvers are hung just under fluorescent lamps, they prevent glare by shielding the lamp from view—you can only see the lamp by looking up into the fixture.

At left is crystal panel #76 with almost clear pattern; at far right #70 with approximately sixteen raised pyramidal prisms per square inch. Both water-white crystal glass panels are made by ASG Industries Inc. In the center is a portion of mirror-surfaced wedged louver, also useful for avoiding direct-view glare from lamps.

Paracube louvers are licensed by the General Electric Company and are made by the American Louver Company. The louvers are available through some building supply firms and from architectural designers. One retail firm has introduced a home-garden light that comes complete with a low profile fixture shielded by a Para-Wedge louver (Marko Co.). The Marko lights come ready to mount on the wall or suspend above a waterproof tray. Model 2400 with two 40-watt lamps is most efficient, but a smaller unit with two 20-watt lamps is available for use in a limited space.

Incandescent Floods and Spots

Tall foliage plants in floor tubs, specimens placed for enjoyment during their flowering period, and built-in planter beds are dramatic when illuminated by overhead incandescent bulbs. For efficiency, bulbs with built-in reflectors or fixtures with incorporated reflectors are better than plain screw-in globes. Duro-Lite Company offers Plant Lite 75-watt R-30 and 150-watt R-40 incandescent bulbs that are formulated to give light high in red tones. The bulbs have a standard, medium screw-in base to fit household fixtures.

If you use these, keep them at least 2 feet above foliage to prevent burn. The Plant Lite incandescent and similar bulbs sold for horticultural use should be thought of as display lamps to supplement daylight for a few hours each day. It is not efficient to grow plants entirely under incandescents. In fact, standard incandescent reflector bulbs are perfectly satisfactory for dramatic night lighting. You need not pay a premium for special plant lights. When foliage plants are largely dependent on artificial light to supplement meager sunlight in dim foyers or dark rooms, the horticultural floods, though decorative and useful, are still not equal to fluorescent tubes in efficiency.

With any of the incandescents it is safest to use ceramic sockets, especially for bulbs over 75-watts.

Efficient and safest for plants are incandescent reflector lamps, which are internally coated to reflect heat toward the bulb base while light shines forward for foliage. General Electric offers the Cool Beam bulb and Sylvania has a similar bulb called Cool Lux, available in 75- or 150-watt. Both brands must be used in heat resistant porcelain sockets. Where water may splash on light bulbs, as in a porch, basement, or greenhouse situation, use an *outdoor* fixture with waterproof bulbs, for example, the Sylvania 150-watt PAR-38 bulb which has a rated life of 2000 hours. Most manufacturers rate 75- to 150-watt reflector bulbs around 2000 life-hours, which is considerably less burning time than the 20,000 hour listed life of rapid-start 40-watt fluorescent tubes. However the dramatic directional lighting of reflector incandescents cannot be duplicated by fluorescents.

Theatrical Effects

The ultimate in dramatic lighting can be produced with a light fixture modeled after movie and television lights, as seen in the photograph of Berkey Colortran Showlites. These sturdy

The Mini Pro Showlite of Berkey Colortran uses 100-watt tungsten halogen bulbs. Adjustable barndoors permit precise control of the light spill. The same fixture is available in a model that fits into ceiling tracks. (Berkey Colortran photo)

home models of professional spotlights provide a strong bright beam, controlled with barn doors or a dimmer if you wish.

Since the quartz lamps are rather hot and the beam is concentrated, be careful to keep plants at least 4 feet away. Closer, the temperature may go high enough to cause foliage damage. At 4 feet the theatrical Showlites raise the temperature 5° to 15°; at 6 feet the rise will hardly be felt. Since these fixtures are designed for mounting on a ceiling or at a wall-ceiling junction, they are usually at least five feet away, even without special planning.

4
Custom-Designed Light Gardens

An excellent location for the display of plants in a light garden is a bookcase, sure to be found in at least one or two rooms of your house or apartment. A major advantage of bookcase gardens is that a shelf or two of plants under lights provides illumination in what would otherwise be a solid wall of books.

Living Art

Light gardens can be a form of living art where you work with nature in creating a constantly changing picture of exotic beauty. What painting can give you this? Actually I find that artworks, sculptures and carvings for example, blend with plants to their mutual enhancement.

A skillfully arranged bookcase garden, set amid your favorite volumes, perhaps with some speakers (for your listening pleasure, not the plants'!), will always be attractive.

Construction

Installing a light garden in an existing bookcase requires very little work. Cover the five interior surfaces with decorator

A self-standing light garden suits any decorating plan, has two 40-watt lamps, here lighting a collection of begonias and gesneriads with an ivy at front left where the light is dim.

Tall plants like this tree azalea respond to supplemental light from overhead incandescents, useful to illuminate the flowers at night. Large plants in small pots must be watered often when in bloom or growth.

white or a similar flat paint. If you want another shade behind or to the side of your plants, select a light-toned pastel. Dark colors do not reflect light back onto lower leaves. One technique I use in our living room is to put a mirror behind the plants. The mirror visually doubles the lovely display.

Fixtures

Purchase strip fixtures of appropriate size. It is more efficient to use one 48-inch fixture for 40-watt tubes than to place two 20-watt fixtures end to end. Compact strip fixtures will project out from the mounting shelf 3½ to 4½ inches, depending on the brand you buy. For a finished appearance, drill holes at the top of each shelf and run the fixture wires behind the bookcase or inside a cabinet. (You can conceal a timer behind books or inside a cabinet shelf.)

Install a narrow valance of wood or Plexiglas (available in many colors) across the top front shelf opening, thus shielding the actual lamp from view. If you wish to present a framed garden effect, continue the valance material around all four sides. This will hide most of the pots, too. If your room is very dry, install sliding doors of clear Plexiglas across the front of each garden shelf. If the doors are very tight you will have to drill a few vent holes in the door or bookcase wall, unless you

Roscoflex reflection media can be glued or stapled in place, washed, or bent. Shown are "F" flexible film at top, "S" for soft reflection at lower right, "H" in center for sharp direct reflection, and "M" for mirror-like reflection at left center.

want high humidity and tropical temperatures within. An enclosed bookshelf light garden usually provides almost terrarium conditions.

How Many Lamps?

Foliage plants require the least light so they can often subsist under one tube. At the other extreme are high-light requirement orchids and succulents that bloom best under four or more tubes. In between are average houseplants, such as begonias, gesneriads, and assorted flowering subjects that prosper under two or three tubes. When planning a custom-designed light garden, you will find it easy to figure in watts per square foot.

A dull cellar window is here transformed into a bright indoor garden where fluorescent lamps supplement the morning sun. Left to right are *Begonia* 'Aries', *Coleus blumei* hybrid, African-violet, and *Aglaonema commutatum*.

Watts per Square Foot

For example 20-watt tubes are 24 inches long. Flowering African-violets should receive 15–20 watts of light per square foot of growing space. Therefore the popular two-bulb 20-watt fixture works out well by providing adequate light for an area 2 feet long by 1 foot wide. (2 feet long x 1 foot wide = 2 square feet x 20 watts per foot = 40 watts or the standard two-bulb 20-watt growing lamp.)

General Requirements

To plan a custom light garden efficiently, figure on these general requirements of minimum lamp watts per square foot:

Foliage Plants: 10 to 15 watts per square foot, with lamps 6 to 15 inches away.
Flowering Plants: 15 to 20 watts per square foot, 6 to 10 inches away.

These measurements are for most of the popular houseplants, including flowering begonias, gesneriads, and similar medium-light requirement species.

High Light

Orchids, most bromeliads, flowering geraniums, cactus and many other succulents need 20 to 30 watts per square foot, 8 to 12 inches away. For example, a 40-watt reflector fixture with four tubes will give adequate light for these plants in a bookcase garden or similar situation with white surroundings over an area of 4 feet by about 1½ feet.

Seed starting, cuttings for propagation, and rooting leaves—situations where plants are under lamps for short periods—can be managed with 10–15 watts per square foot, the lamps 4 to 6 inches away. The distance between rooting or seed flats and lamps is easily increased by using blocks of plastic foam or inverted pots.

Increased Light

In most applications you may furnish more watts per square foot with the option of having the lamps farther from the foliage. A good rule is to provide as much fluorescent light as any given species will accept without burning, yellowing, or stunting growth.

With maximum intensity, plants will grow compactly and bloom freely. However, for reasons of space or economy most of us cannot count on the extreme intensities used in research growth chambers, nor is it necessary to have so much light to produce sturdy flowering houseplants.

Foliage plants remain in healthy growth when diffuse sun is supplemented with artificial light. This palm gets sun from a skylight, supplemental light from overhead incandescents.

Distance and Intensity

The intensity of a lamp decreases rapidly with distance. It might seem reasonable that a tube giving 500 foot-candles of brightness at one foot would give 250 foot-candles at two feet, but this is not the case. Light follows an inverse square law of diminishing brightness. This means that when you double the distance you reduce the light to one-quarter of its original brightness.

One way of decreasing the effect of light drop-off is to provide surrounding surfaces that reflect much of the light back onto the lower foliage. White or light-colored paints, aluminum foil, and mirrors all help to utilize the total light from lamps.

Mirrors

Covering walls, backs of garden cases, or bookshelves with mirrors creates double beauty by reflecting foliage and flowers. Of equal importance is the light that mirrors bounce back onto

My friend Norman Livingston created an orchid-growing area in his basement with uniquely staged fixtures, each holding four 40-watt broad-spectrum fluorescents. A small fan circulates moist air from wet gravel below.

leaves. Unframed mirrors are available in any size, or you may obtain self-sticking mirror panels that are quickly installed on any clean surface.

Louvers

Plastic cube-pattern louvers permit air circulation, cut only about 10–15 percent of the light, and divert light directly downward. Paracube louvers suspended under fluorescent tubes conceal the lights. Even with high-light intensity from many lamps close together covering a whole ceiling, you can prevent glare by installing custom-cut paracube louvers. One type has a bright mirror finish in gold or silver. Another less expensive sort is made of plain white translucent acrylic.

Safety

Before connecting lamps, check that your wall outlets have sufficient reserve power. Most home outlets can supply several 40-watt fluorescent fixtures, even if the same line (and fuse) supplies other appliances. However, for an extensive wattage load, as might be required for a room-sized light garden or a wall garden with six or more four-lamp 40-watt fixtures (960 watts minimum), it is wise to provide a separate circuit with reserve capacity. Consult an electrician for any required modifications.

Grounds

Three-wire grounding plugs and sockets will reduce your chances of getting a shock. Some light stands, such as the Flora Cart of Tube Craft Company, come with a separate ground wire rather than a three-prong plug. Attach one end of the ground wire to the cart frame, then firmly wire or screw the other end to a radiator or waterpipe.

Sockets for incandescent bulbs are supplied in some fluorescent fixtures. If you do not plan to use these sockets, put electric or gaffer's tape over the openings. Even if you avoid splashing water into these sockets, it is highly possible that you might touch the electrically live metal while grooming your plants.

Benches and Tables

For a basement or spare-room light garden, where houseplants are simply grown rather than displayed, the light fixtures above and tables below may be more utilitarian than decorative. One way to construct inexpensive tables is with sawhorse stands that hold plain wooden planks. You can obtain metal sawhorse braces that hold two-by-four-foot lumber and thus quickly erect an easy support for shelves. Allow one support per 4 feet.

Wood Treatment

Paint wood with Cuprinol preservative or a similar product that is labeled "harmless to plants." The preservative will stop rot, mildew, and termites. Cuprinol is available in clear (No. 20), with a green tint (No. 10), or with a brown tint (No. 70). Paint wood, then permit painted sections to dry at least 48 hours before placing plants in the light garden.

Cement Treatment

Paint cement block walls with white road-marking paint or another sort of non-toxic product that will be waterproof when dry. A white or pastel color will reflect light back onto the plants and help utilize all available energy. Another satisfactory treatment for cement or cinder-block surfaces is to cover them with aluminum or mirrorized Mylar, tacked on a wooden frame or pasted up with Elmer's glue.

Tiered Garden

You can turn a basement, spare room, or heated garage into an efficient light garden by constructing a basic H-frame on which you place shelves of ¾-inch exterior plywood for plants. Pots are placed on trays, which can be custom-made of metal, plastic, or fiberglass, or purchased ready-to-use.

Keep the trays filled with moist gravel or coarse perlite to provide humidity around foliage. Hang fixtures with flat white or aluminum reflectors above each shelf. The height between lamps and foliage is adjustable by changing the length of chain supporting each fixture. In a basement or unfinished garage the H-frame is easily supported by nailing the two-by-fours to overhead joists. Where there are no exposed joists or beams the frame must be attached to the ceiling directly, usually with two-by-fours which are first nailed flat along the ceiling into a stud.

If you want to construct an H-frame garden without nailing into ceiling or floor, you can hold the frame with spring-loaded Timber Toppers. These unique devices fit over two-by-threes and, with spring action, hold them snugly against floor and ceiling. (They are made by the Brewster Corporation, Old Saybrook, Connecticut 06475.) When Timber Toppers are used for fixtures more than 24 inches long, I suggest fastening a crosspiece of two-by-three-foot wood diagonally at each end of the H-frame for better overall stability.

In the original line drawing, courtesy of the Sylvania Lighting Center, the H-frame light garden shows 48- to 50-inch two-lamp 40-watt fluorescent fixtures. However, you can modify this feature to fit available space, always using the longest lamp possible for top efficiency. For example, the fixtures could be 96-inch types, high-output models (which require special installation), or the much smaller 24-inch fixtures with 20-watt lamps. Since the fluorescent ballasts will provide some heat, you can grow plants that prefer higher temperatures on the two top tiers.

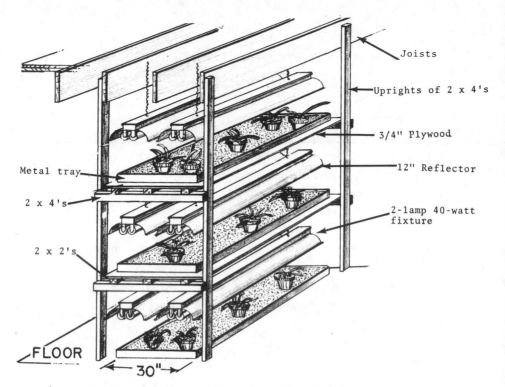

Joists

Uprights of 2 x 4's

3/4" Plywood

12" Reflector

Metal tray

2 x 4's

2-1amp 40-watt
fixture

2 x 2's

FLOOR

30"

An easy-to-construct H-frame light garden is ideal for a basement area.

(Georgia-Pacific photo)

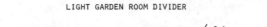

Plans courtesy of **Georgia-Pacific** / **Johnson WAX**

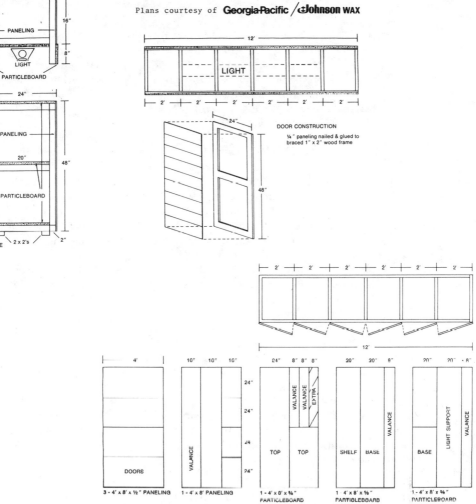

This custom-built light garden was designed to serve as a wall-to-wall room divider. The plans, created by designers of Georgia-Pacific and Johnson Wax, call for a single 8-foot lamp. But for maximum bloom on a wide range of tropical plants, I would install two lamps, preferably wide-spectrum horticultural kinds, such as Wide-Spectrum Gro-Lux. Herbs and foliage plants will grow satisfactorily with the one 8-foot lamp shown in the drawing. For protection of the Spring Green Carousel paneling, give an occasional treatment with Regard, a wax preparation available in liquid or aerosol form. Although plants in the photograph are seen set on the painted particle board counter, you will have less problem with split water and low humidity if all plants are placed on moist gravel or perlite in trays. Plastic trays are available from several mail-order firms listed in Chapter 21. For a more finished appearance, a metal- or fiberglass-lined tray might be custom built for the space available.

INSTRUCTIONS: The measurements and procedures suggested for this light-garden room divider are basic guides but can be adjusted as required to conform to your specific room dimensions. The original plan indicates the light garden to be used as a wall-to-wall room divider, but it can also serve as an island with one end exposed. The open end could be covered with cork to be used as a bulletin board or finished with a Plexiglas acrylic sheet to let soft light through.

CONSTRUCTION: This light garden consists a large "box" base cabinet 12 feet long, 4 feet high, and 2 feet wide, supported on a pair of 2 x 2-inch runners recessed 2 inches from the face to provide toe room beneath the unit. It is easier to paint the components before installation. The top surface, which will be subjected to moisture, should receive several coats of good quality paint on both faces and all edges. You might consider having it covered in Formica, tiles, or Solarium floor covering, especially if the total counter will not be hidden by trays.

Assemble the base first, starting with the seven framework ribs as indicated in the plans. The first and seventh units are positioned on top of the 2 x 2's and nailed into place, then attached to end walls. Next the remaining ribs are positioned on 2-foot centers. Now add the particleboard base, shelf, and top sections. The doors are 4 x 2-foot factory-finished Spring Green Carousel panels, nailed and glued to a 1 x 2 lumber framework, then painted along framework edges and panel backs.

A valance of particleboard is shown, but this can also be made of clear or colored Plexiglas that will let some light come through. I would have the light fixture controlled by a timer to simplify daily on/off functions. A two-lamp F96 strip fixture with 75-watt, 96-inch long Wide-Spectrum Gro-Lux lamps will provide suitable light quality and quantity for most houseplants. The single-lamp fixture, indicated in the plans, is sufficient for foliage or flowering plants on brief display.

MATERIAL LIST:

226 Linear feet of 2 x 2-inch lumber framing
     6 pieces 12 feet long (base runner, base horizontal framing)
     14 pieces 4 feet long base vertical framing)
     21 pieces 2 feet long (base shelf and top frame)
     28 pieces 2 feet long (valance frame)
3 pieces 4 x 8, 5/8-inch Georgia-Pacific particleboard (base, shelves, top, valance)
3 pieces 4 x 8, ¼-inch Georgia-Pacific Spring Green Carousel paneling or paneling to suit your decorating plan (12 doors, 48 x 24 inches each)
1 piece 4 x 8, ¼-inch Georgia-Pacific Spring Green Carousel paneling or similar paneling to match your selection for doors (valance panel)
168 linear feet of 1 x 2-inch lumber door framing (24 pieces 4 feet long, 36 pieces 2 feet long)

2 pieces 1½-inch by 12-foot batten strips for vertical accent pieces
1 8-foot lamp fixture (see notes above regarding number of lamps)
Hardware:
    6 pair door pulls
    12 pair 2½-inch hinges
    12 pair magnetic catches (to hold doors shut)
    Nails, adhesive, putty stick, paint etc.

Situations

This basic design is useful where you need considerable storage space—in the kitchen or den, against a garage wall, adjacent to a sun porch, in a greenhouse, or between kitchen and dining room.

5
The Quality of Light

Controlled experiments and practical findings in home light gardens confirm that the *quality* of light, that is the band of colors called the spectrum, is as important to plants as the *intensity* or quantity of light. Previously growers believed that brightness alone was the primary factor in determining whether their houseplants would prosper and bloom. Now we understand that green plants need certain colors of light to initiate normal cycles in growth and blooming.

The Right Rays

The blue and red rays in the visible spectrum are essential for photosynthesis. Through this complicated process, plants with chlorophyll (the green coloring matter) capture light energy and transform it into an organic form of stored energy for growth. For this process to occur with optimum efficiency, plants require adequate and balanced light

Growth Cues

Of the near-visible spectrum, far-red light is also important for sturdy growth. Subtle variations in wave length and

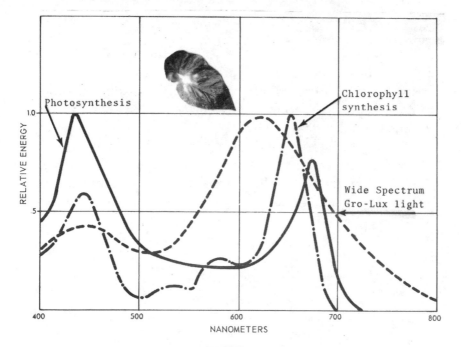

The spectrum output of Sylvania's Wide-Spectrum Gro-Lux (dashed line) is in good agreement with the parts of the spectrum most used by plants for photosynthesis (solid line), and chlorophyll synthesis (dot/dash line). (Diagram is based on a chart from GTE Sylvania)

ENERGY EMISSION IN ARBITRARY COLOR BANDS
40 WATT FLUORESCENT LAMPS
In Watts and Percent of Total Emission

	BAND IN NANOMETERS	WARM WHITE		COOL WHITE		STANDARD GRO-LUX		GRO-LUX/WS	
		WATTS	PERCENT	WATTS	PERCENT	WATTS	PERCENT	WATTS	PERCENT
Ultra Violet	< 380	0.13	1.52	0.16	1.68	0.10	1.42	0.27	3.16
Violet	380-430	0.46	5.15	0.72	7.57	0.70	9.67	1.07	12.48
Blue	430-490	1.15	12.91	1.98	20.78	1.96	27.07	1.22	14.29
Green	490-560	1.80	20.24	2.35	24.67	1.02	14.02	1.24	14.49
Yellow	560-590	2.06	23.17	1.74	18.27	0.10	1.42	0.83	9.77
Orange	590-630	2.13	23.95	1.69	17.75	0.44	6.05	1.36	15.93
Red	630-700	1.03	11.53	0.81	8.47	2.86	39.55	1.86	21.78
Far-Red	700-780	0.13	1.53	0.07	0.81	0.06	0.80	0.69	8.10
TOTAL		8.89	100.00	9.52	100.00	7.24	100.00	8.54	100.00

(Chart by GTE Sylvania)

combinations of various colors (blue with red, for example) interreact to enhance photosynthesis. Laboratory research has discovered in green plants a light-sensitive pigment called phytochrome. This pigment is cued or activated by slight changes in red and far-red light.

One wavelength of red light programs the phytochrome to encourage maturation, ripening, and dormancy, while a slightly different part of the red spectrum (far-red and invisible infrared) signals cell activity, thus stimulating plant growth and new foliage.

Indoor Light

Artificial lights, to induce optimum development, must contain the required spectrum. Sunlight contains all the necessary light rays plus other portions of the spectrum not so important to plants, or so tests to date lead us to believe. The green and yellow portions of light, although most important in human vision, are not so important to green plants. Research by U.S.D.A. scientists indicates that it is mainly the blue rays that promote foliage growth and the red rays that foster flowering.

New Lamps

Manufacturers of fluorescent tubes have employed these findings and those of their own independent research to develop lamps formulated to enhance plant growth. By combining various rare powdered chemicals (phosphors), they can customize the spectrum of a fluorescent lamp and thereby create a color balance of maximum value to plants.

The horticultural lamps are higher in output of blue and red rays than are common household lamps, such as Cool White. The Gro-Lux lamps, for example, have about three times more usable red energy than Cool White lamps.

Survey of Lamps

Lighting companies, such as Duro-Lite, General Electric, GTE Sylvania, and Westinghouse, have all produced versions of standard household fluorescents, the Cool White and Daylight lamps. These are the tubes most often used in office and home fixtures. Variations of these popular lamp colors include Deluxe and Warm White lamps, designed to show more flattering skin tones.

Cool White is visually brightest, Daylight the bluest, Warm White nearest to incandescent bulb colors. Those tubes with a spectrum tailored to plants are made by many of the same lighting companies that offer standard household lamps. The horticultural lamps are of two general types; the standard rosy-hued kinds, such as the original Gro-Lux, and the newer broad-spectrum types.

Exacum affine 'Midget' (rear) and *Peperomia* 'Little Fantasy' show variations when grown under different light sources. The largest plants, formed under Wide-Spectrum Gro-Lux, also bloomed freely. The most compact growth, but with fewer flowers, was under the standard Gro-Lux. Vita-Lite, with the same color light as sun, produced plants of an in-between size.

GRO-LUX   VITA-LITE   WS GRO-LUX

Rivina humilis, a tropical herb known as rouge-plant for deep red color of its fruit, produced the most flowers under the Wide-Spectrum Gro-Lux lamp.

Rosy-Hued Lamps

Sylvania's Gro-Lux is a widely used warm-toned horticultural lamp, popular for seed starting and for many medium-light requirement plants. It is excellent for enhancing colors, since reds and pinks turn into unusual vibrant hues not seen under other lamps or in daylight. Similar, but less pink in color, is the original Westinghouse Plant-Gro lamp. The newer Westinghouse plant light, Agro-Lite, is slightly pinkish but has a broader spectrum than the older Plant-Gro.

Broad-Spectrum Tubes

The most recent horticultural development in fluorescent lamps has been the creation of broad-spectrum tubes. Currently available are Agro-Lite (Westinghouse Electric

Corp.), Natur-Escent (Duro-Lite Inc.), Verilux TruBloom (Verilux Co.), Vita-Lite (Duro-Lite Inc.), and Wide-Spectrum Gro-Lux (GTE Sylvania).

All but Agro-Lite and Wide-Spectrum Gro-Lux have a color range (kelvin) equal to noon sunlight. The Verilux and Vita-Lite lamps were developed for industrial, decorative, and medical markets, but recently have been offered for use in home light gardens. Since their light is the color of noon daylight, you can hardly see their light when it supplements sun at a window. Daylight color film captures nearly normal tones when exposed with Verilux TruBloom and Vita-Lite lamps.

Vita-Lite has more ultraviolet than Duro-Lite's similar Natur-Escent. Growers of high-light requirement succulents and bromeliads report good bloom and excellent foliage color under Vita-Lites. I find them useful for orchids. A twisted 40-watt lamp is available, too, with about 10 percent more light.

Wide-Spectrum Gro-Lux lamps cost but a few cents more than Cool White tubes which makes them the least expensive horticultural fluorescent. I consider the Wide Spectrum Gro-Lux an excellent buy and they give me fine results with a broad range of tropical plants, including orchids, begonias, and many succulents.

Agro-Lite of Westinghouse is the most recently introduced lamp developed for plants. To our eyes the color resembles Wide-Spectrum Gro-Lux, a slightly warmer tone than daylight but quite pleasing. Just as important is what the plants "see," which parts of the spectrum are available in Agro-Lites.

These new tubes were created after testing various types of fluorescents; they are specifically formulated to provide high energy in sections of the spectrum most utilized by green plants, that is, violet–blue and orange–red. I have been growing houseplants under Agro-Lites and find the lamps excellent, producing compact growth, healthy color, and good flowering.

Leaves of the gesneriad *Chirita sinensis* blush red under too bright a light. At left, a leaf from a plant 8 inches below a Wide-Spectrum Gro-Lux; at right, 15 inches below the same lamp. The foliage is normal green with silver markings.

Economy

Since the horticultural lamps contain the light most utilized by plants, they are more economical than lamps that produce brightness in unneeded colors. The energy to burn a 40-watt horticultural lamp is the same as that required to operate a 40-watt household Cool White lamp, but the light produced by the Cool White is not nearly as well utilized by flowering plants.

Combinations

Before broad spectrum horticultural fluorescents were available, I combined incandescent bulbs with standard household Cool White lamps to get the far-red rays not found in the common fluorescents. A ratio of two 15- to 25-watt bulbs per two 40-watt fluorescents is successful in providing enough red rays for sturdy plant growth with Cool White lamps. If the plants are at least 8 inches away, 40-watt incandescent bulbs can be used, but there is always danger of burn from incandescent bulbs since they are so much hotter than fluorescents.

When horticultural tubes were introduced, I elected to use them and thus eliminated the hot incandescents. This also resulted in a saving on the electric bill. There remain few reasons for using incandescent bulbs mixed with fluorescents, but you should understand what values the incandescents do have.

Incandescent Values

Incandescent bulbs combined with standard Gro-Lux or Plant Gro fluorescents, at a ratio of 30 to 40 incandescent watts to 80 watts of fluorescent light, grow more floriferous African-violets than fluorescent lamps alone. When Cool White fluorescents are used for plant growing it is important to add the incandescent bulbs to achieve maximum flowering. For foliage plants the incandescents are not necessary, even with Cool White/Warm White lamps.

Incandescent bulbs are easily utilized in modern fluorescent fixtures that can be ordered with sockets for incandescents placed between the tubes. The usual arrangement has two incandescent sockets per fixture.

Increased Bulb Life

By using the incandescent bulbs, rated to burn at 130 volts, you will increase bulb life since electric fixtures in our country receive 110–120 volts. The red rays are still effective from the bulbs made for 130 volts, but the bulbs last much longer.

Heat

Sometimes the heat given off by incandescent bulbs is an advantage for plants in cool environments. However heat is usually a nuisance in confined growth chambers, bookshelf gardens, or small rooms. Plants do not do well if kept too warm and any plant part touching an incandescent bulb will quickly burn. In contrast, some plants can touch fluorescent lamps in the cooler center section without immediate danger of burning.

Although incandescent bulbs help grow better plants than when standard household or limited spectrum fluorescents are used alone, incandescents are not necessary when you use the newer broad-spectrum fluorescents. The full-spectrum lamps (Wide-Spectrum Gro-Lux, Agro-Lite, etc.) contain enough far-red light for normal growth and blooming of most houseplants.

Standard Fluorescents

Many home-light gardeners are satisfied with the flowering of medium-to low-light requirement plants grown under standard Cool White, Daylight, and Warm White tubes. A favorite combination for African-violets and other gesneriads is one Cool White and one Warm White. An advantage in using these widely available tubes is that they are about one-third the price of the horticultural fluorescents. The only horticultural tube that is almost as low in price as Cool Whites is Sylvania's Wide-Spectrum Gro-Lux.

Cool White and Warm White lamps are also brighter than horticultural lamps so they are doubly useful in dark places where lights must serve as illumination for decoration, safety, and plant growing.

Low-light requirement foliage species, such as ferns, philodendrons, and ivies have done just as well for me and many other gardeners, under Cool White and Warm White tubes as under the more expensive broad-spectrum fluo-

Impatiens 'Scarlet Ripple' produced acceptable plants under several types of fluorescents but had the most flowers on bushy plants under broad-spectrum horticultural lamps.

rescents. This is not true of flowering plants, so lamp choice is ultimately influenced by the species you wish to grow.

Supplemental Light

The type of fluorescent tube used is less important when the artificial light is only to supplement sunlight. At a window, in a greenhouse, or bright sunroom where plants get the major portion of light from the sun (and thus receive the full spectrum), fluorescent supplemental lighting can be effective in standard Cool White/Warm White or related deluxe types that are slightly warmer in color.

If you wish to match supplemental light with daylight, choose one of the lamps balanced for noon daylight color, such as Vita-Lite or Verilux TruBloom. They increase brightness and extend light-hours without altering the natural color of midday sun.

Lumens

Manufacturer's specifications indicate the actual brightness of fluorescent tubes in *lumens.* Light output from fluorescents

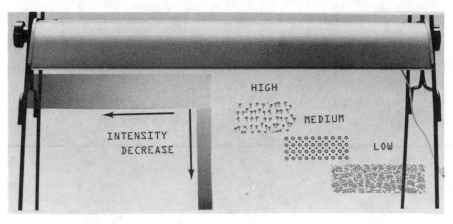

Since light intensity from fluorescents decreases toward the ends of the tubes and as the distance from the lamp increases, plant species should be placed according to their brightness requirements. Plants that need most light are placed at the center of the tubes, those that need the least are grown toward the ends and along the edges of the lighted area.

drops fastest during the first 100 hours of use, so companies traditionally publish figures showing effective brightness *after* 100 hours.

A sample of 40-watt tubes shows the General Electric Cool White Lamp with a light output of 3200 lumens, the Verilux with 2168 lumens, and a Sylvania Daylight tube with 2600 lumens. Sylvania lists no lumens for Gro-Lux lamps.

The lumen figure shows only what a lamp is giving off in brightness. How much of the light actually reaches the plants depends on reflector size and color, distance between lamps, and between lamps and foliage. Light measured at the plant position, the actual light *received* by the foliage, is measured in foot-candles. These measurements show only brightness. Fluorescent lamp color (the spectrum) is also an important factor in the efficiency of a tube as shown by tests mentioned earlier.

Foot-candles

The brightness at any distance from a light source is traditionally given in foot-candles, a measurement of visible light, easily made with a foot-candle meter or converted from readings on a sophisticated photographic light meter. The more foot-candles shown, the brighter the light. Foot-candles measurement is important in estimating adequate illumination for work areas, and in creating proper contrast ratios in photography or television recording.

How Bright

Since brightness is only one of several important factors in growing houseplants under lights, you will not find foot-candle measurements of much value. Watts per square foot, observation, and tube type are more practical considerations. Nevertheless since light intensity is important, you may notice variations in plant response under different fluorescent lamps. Some of the difference will be due to brightness. For example, the brightness range between three popular fluorescent lamps shows that Cool White tubes have more visible light, which can be measured in foot-candles, and thus the Cool White tubes look brighter. The standard Gro-Lux tube, which has a rosy glow, is only 34 percent as bright, and the Wide-Spectrum Gro-Lux is 72 percent as bright as Cool White.

Where brightness is a significant factor, as for succulents or high-light requirement orchids, I still prefer the dimmer Wide-Spectrum Gro-Lux or similar broad-spectrum lamps for their improved light spectrums.

To obtain maximum brightness, put plants slightly closer to the horticultural lamps, or set the tubes closer together, thus providing more watts per square foot. A 2- to 4-inch space between lamps is efficient.

Practical Approach

The color of light in different fluorescent tubes is not measured equally by photographic or foot-candle meters that are sensitive mainly to visible light. This means that the reading of the energy values useful to green plants can be off by a significant percentage. This variation of foot-candle measurements for horticulture is avoided in research labs where a special meter is employed to determine *actual* Spectral Energy Distribution (SED) curves of fluorescent lamps.

I include some charts showing the SED curves of fluorescents, as background information for the curious, but you *do not have to understand this data to grow houseplants under lights!*

The multitude of factors that influence healthy growth include heat, light color, light intensity, day-length, night-length, temperature, air circulation, *et al.* The following points present a more practical system of measuring suitable light intensity for your plants.

Observation

After more than twenty years of growing thousands of species under lights, I know that you will have success if you follow these guidelines:

1. Arrange lamps 4 to 12 inches above foliage in fixtures with at least two tubes and a bright white or aluminum reflector. A 40-watt tube is more efficient than two 20-watts.

2. Use horticultural fluorescents or combinations of broad-spectrum horticultural lamps with Cool White lamps for best results with a wide variety of flowering plants.

3. Set an automatic timer to provide 14 to 16 hours of light per 24 hours, reduced to 12 hours for eight weeks in early winter.

4. Provide environmental conditions required by the species you wish to grow—usually relative humidity 40 to 60

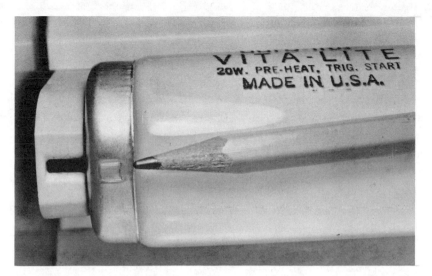

For maximum life, set the lamps in fixtures with the guide-crease directly in line with the socket opening.

percent and a temperature in the 60's at night, into high 70's during light hours.

Close observation of your plants will cue you to any changes necessary. Slight yellowing of foliage or excessively compact growth are indications that light intensity is too strong. The solution is to increase distance between plants and lamps.

Sparse blooming on normally floriferous species, very deep green foliage, or leggy drawn-out growth show that light intensity is too low. The solution is to move lamps closer to the plants, perhaps increase the number of lamps if you are using only one or two tubes.

Lamp Condition

New lamps are brighter than those that have burned 75 to 100 hours. Therefore new lamps can be placed somewhat farther above foliage than older lamps. For example, if ferns or African-violets have prospered for a year with lamps 10 inches above foliage and you replace the lamps all at once, move the fixture 4 to 6 inches higher for the first 75–100 hours of use.

Another system is to keep lamp-to-foliage distance constant but replace tubes one at a time over a period of weeks. This works for fixtures with two to six tubes and guards against sudden yellowing of leaves.

Relative Measurement

You can apply an accurate measuring system to light gardening through use of a photographic light meter. You need not measure foot-candles. Instead determine a repeatable standard indication of suitable light levels, using any available meter.

Light Meter Use

Once you determine that a given foliage-to-lamp distance is successful for healthy growth and flowering under your conditions make notes of these facts:

1. Write down the tube type (Wide-Spectrum Gro-Lux, Vita-Lite, or whatever) and the wattage.

2. Take a measurement with your light meter, reading reflected light off the palm of your hand, held at the same level as your healthy plants. You can also measure the light with an incident reading that collects the light coming from the tube. (See meter instruction booklet.) Write down whatever value is expressed on your meter. For example, if your meter needle goes to Number eight, write that down.

3. In the future, to determine if a given area has sufficient light for healthy growth under your conditions, just

repeat precisely the meter-reading techniques you previously used.

This technique is most precise when you are dealing with the same plants in all situations, but it can also provide useful indications for different species that have the same general light requirements. After growing several generations of tropicals under fluorescents, you will be able to arrange fixtures without concern for perfect measurements.

Plants for Different Light Intensities

LOW. A single lamp or dim daylight supplemented with fluorescents or overhead incandescents.

> *Aglaonema* (Chinese evergreens)
> *Aspidistra elatior* (Cast-iron plant)
> Ferns
> Philodendrons
> *Pothos* (Devil's Ivy)
> *Selaginella*

MEDIUM. Two 20-watt fluorescents, about 10–15 watts per square foot of growing space, or toward ends of fixtures.

> African-violets
> *Anthurium*
> *Begonia, B. bowerae* and Rex hybrids
> *Caladium*
> *Cissus* (Grape-ivy)
> *Ficus*, ornamental figs
> *Hedera helix*, ivies
> *Paphiopedilum*, orchids
> *Spathiphyllum*

HIGH. Three or more lamps, or bright daylight supplemented with broad-spectrum tubes.

> *Agave* (Century plants)
> *Aloe*
> Begonias for flowers: *semperflorens*, Angelwings, etc.
> Bromeliads
> Cattleya-type orchids, compact species and hybrids
> *Epidendrums*, orchids
> *Euphorbia* (Crown-of-thorn and succulent sorts)
> Geraniums

Fluorescent Tube Life

Fluorescent tubes normally continue to glow for several years, even on 14-hour light cycles. However, after about 5000 hours of burning the tubes begin to loose enough brightness to affect plant growth. When plants are dependent on fluorescents for their total light requirement, change lamps every year or between 5000 and 6000 hours, sooner if tubes blacken abnormally at the ends. Where fluorescents are employed to supplement sunlight you can count on two to three years of life, but if finances permit, it is better to replace lamps no later than every two years.

Power Problems

During summer brown-outs, when electric power companies in the Northeast were forced to reduce (or sometimes cut completely) their power output for days at a time, I noticed that fluorescents in my greenhouse often failed to light, especially when temperatures went above 80°. With the same reduction in power, but under cooler conditions, the fluorescents in my basement light gardens functioned normally.

This illustrates two factors in the average life of fluorescent lamps:

1. Tubes last longer when power supplies are neither too high nor too low. Fluctuations in voltage shorten lamp life.

2. Excessive heat shortens tube life and can also cause ballasts to burn out or fail long before they would normally.

Solutions

If tubes blacken prematurely because of voltage variations, they should be replaced. You might be able to turn off fluorescent fixtures during periods of voltage variation (especially reductions in power), both to save electricity and to prevent shortened tube life.

Growth chambers, each with a different type of light inside, at the Beltsville, Maryland U.S.D.A. Research Station.

Transfer plants to bright windows but with care to avoid direct midday sun that might burn foliage. In the warmer months light-garden plants can go outside under high shade, on a porch, or in a lath house.

Tube Placement

Rapid-start tubes have an indentation or guide crease on the metal lamp base. This mark should be directly centered in the socket opening when tubes are correctly seated in the fixtures. If the guide crease is *not* directly opposite the socket opening the lamp pins are not making maximum contact with the socket spring clips. This often leads to shortened lamp life and excessive blackening of the tubes.

Latest Research

Since we still have so much to learn about the complex relationships between green plants, light sources, and the environment, several universities and the U.S.D.A. continue extensive experiments. At the Ornamentals Research Laboratory of the U.S.D.A. in Beltsville, Maryland, I studied the latest research. Dr. Henry M. Cathey, the director, opened chamber after chamber, showing me how various combinations of lamps kept tomatoes, marigolds, lettuce, and other plants alive.

Most successful in the growth chambers were plants under low-pressure sodium (SOX) lamps combined with some incandescent bulbs. With this lighting, plants look gray; Dr. Cathey acknowledges that the most *efficient* growth lights are not the most aesthetically *pleasing*. In a functional basement light garden the strange color from sodium lamps may not be important, but I would not want sodium lamps in a living area since they make the skin look gray and green foliage appear almost white!

Incandescent bulbs and low-pressure sodium lamps provide about 2,500 foot-candles of illumination for tomato, marigold, and lettuce plants inside a growth chamber at U.S.D.A. Research Station.

Reflective Values

Dr. Cathey's research confirms my own observations regarding the value of highly reflective material around plants under lights. Because the sun shines from the sky, we need not be limited to supplying artificial light from above only. I use aluminum foil, white gravel, or perlite and paint all nearby surfaces white or cover them with insulation grade foil. Similar

Giving houseplants as much sun as possible lets you save energy by reducing the amount of artificial light required for sturdy growth. Here shelves are of clear Plexiglas; plants that need most light (geraniums) are at the top just below the overhead fixtures; species with lower-light requirements are underneath. Plexiglas is easily cleaned with a mild detergent and will not break like glass. (Rohm and Hass Co. photo)

results are obtained with mirrored Mylar, or Roscoflex reflection media (Rosco Labs), everything arranged to bounce light back onto lower leaves, thus utilizing the total light output.

Top Efficiency

Pure research often produces results that have limited applicability to home-hobby situations, but some findings do give us clues for using artificial light efficiently:

A. Utilize available sunlight along with fluorescents.

B. Provide highly reflective surfaces to bounce light onto foliage.

C. Maintain the highest light intensity practical by changing lamps every twelve to fourteen months and keeping lamps clean.

D. Set plants close to the tubes to gain full benefit of brightness.

Plants in your home usually react differently from lab specimens in controlled growth chambers. The ultimate test in tube type or light-hours is made under your *own* growing conditions.

6
Night Into Day

The plants you select will determine how many hours per day the lamps will burn, and at what time you choose to provide light. For living-room planters, room dividers, and display areas, time lights to coincide with human activity. For most houseplants, light hours can reach 16 to 18 hours per day without reducing flower production. Even where some daylight reaches plants, you can safely set fluorescents to come on an hour after sunrise and still enjoy illuminated beauty until nine or ten o'clock at night.

Light-hours change gradually from season to season, but you need not follow nature's variations with astronomical precision. Adjusting your timers two or three times a year to reflect variations in natural light hours is sufficient. If you enjoy fitting light hours to nature's pattern, you can obtain sophisticated timers that adjust precisely every day throughout the year. However such an expensive device is not required for success with houseplants under lights.

Dark Spots

When light gardens receive no sunlight at all you can have "daytime" occur anywhere within a 24-hour cycle. If your daily work precludes gardening in your basement until evening, simply set timers to begin "day" around ten or eleven o'clock in the morning. Then every evening the lights will stay on until late in *your* day, an automatic method of combining gardening pleasure with a nine to five career.

Biorhythms

It might be easy to give exact do and don't rules for plants under lights, but so many environmental factors determine growth and blooming that dogmatic directions are unreliable. Fortunately favorite houseplants are so adaptable that we can follow certain guidelines and achieve rewarding success. We can adjust environmental factors bit by bit until we reach the optimum balance under our conditions for the species we are growing.

Day-Length Means Night-Length

When the light reactions of plants were first studied, it was thought that day-length was the important factor. Later research proved that it is the night-length or total number of dark hours per 24-hour cycle that triggers most flowering reactions.

Basic Divisions

Plants were grouped into four photoperiod groups by W. W. Garner and H. A. Allard, the government scientists who studied plant reactions to day-length. Species that bloom over a wide range of day- and night-lengths are *indeterminate* (sometimes called *day-neutral*). Among the indetermediate are most of the houseplants we grow, which makes light gardening all the more flexible. Day-length intermediates bloom well only when the light and dark periods are equal. The New

Guinea *Impatiens* and *Bougainvillea* are some of the few indetermediate day-length houseplants.

The *short-day* plants include those that must have 13–14-hour nights to initiate flower buds. These include the pointsettia and winter-flowering *Kalanchoe blossfeldiana* hybrids.

Long-day (short-night) plants bloom when days are more than 14 hours long. Summer-blooming species, including tuberous begonias, most annuals, and the charming Persian-violet (*Exacum affine*) are long-day plants.

Photoperiods

The light rhythms of green plants are called photoperiods. Among ornamental plants are these examples of short-day (long-night), long-day (short-night), and day-neutral or indeterminate cultivars:

LONG-NIGHT (10–12 light-hours):
Aphelandra squarrosa (Zebra plant)
Begonia, Christmas and winter-blooming
Some *Cattleya, Dendrobium*, and *Phalaenopsis*, orchids
Chrysanthemums
Euphorbia pulcherrima, poinsettia
Gardenias
Kalanchoe blossfeldiana (seedlings grow well with 16-hour days)
Sixifraga (Strawberry-geranium) stolonifera (*Syn. sarmentosa*) Initiates flowers with long nights, but short nights are satisfactory for foliage.

SHORT-NIGHT (14–18 light-hours):
Begonias, summer-blooming tuberous
Exacum affine (Persian-violet)
Most annuals

INDETERMINATE (12–18 light hours):
African-violets and other gesneriads
Begonia semperflorens hybrids
Coleus
Geraniums
Marigold hybrids. Produce flowers with 12–16 hour days, but tests show growth is fuller with 16–hour days.
Miniature Roses

If 14 Is Good Then 24 Must Be. . . .

Indoor plants, especially those dependent on artificial light alone, do require at least 10 hours of bright light for sturdy growth. For most, 14 to 18 hours of light per 24-hour period will let them grow and bloom with ease. However, just because 14 hours may be a good day-length, it does not mean that 24 hours is better. In fact tomato seedlings can be killed by successive periods of constant light. Giving more light than necessary also wastes electricity and, of course, costs more for power and lamp replacements.

The only houseplant that some experiments indicate is able to grow normally under 24 hours of light is the African-violet, but since 14–18 hours would provide just as many flowers you waste energy by giving more light-hours. Actually, nothing is gained by giving 24 hours of light per day to any of your houseplants. Instead, try supplementing daylight with a few hours of early to mid-evening illumination. For example, a philodendron or African-violet under a reading lamp will do better if the lamp is on from sunset until nine or ten o'clock at night; but remember to turn off the light when you go to bed. Your plants need sleep too.

Long-Day Benefits

Seedlings benefit from 16- to 18-hour days; they grow faster and bloom sooner as Dr. David G. Leach, famous rhododendron hybridizer, reports in the *American Horticulturist*: "At the end of the first season, rhododendron seedlings which have had supplemental fluorescent light to produce a 16-hour growing day, are about two and one half times larger than those which have had a natural dawn-to-dusk day of growth following germination."

My own experience with hundreds of orchids and other tropical plants confirms that accelerated growth can be obtained when seedlings are given supplemental light to increase day-length. Thus in the greenhouse I use fluorescent lamps to extend the short winter days, and many plants bloom sooner than if they were dependent on sunlight. This is important when you are growing orchids, anthuriums, bromeliads, amaryllis, and other species that normally required three or more years to bloom.

When the seedlings reach maturity I gradually reduce day-length until they are under 12 to 13 hours of light per 24–hour period. This extended night, often coupled with dark-hour temperatures 5 to 10 degrees lower than for young seedlings, helps plants initiate flowering.

Another way to accomplish this on plants grown outdoors in the summer is to leave them outside until the nights approach

---

These original furniture designs by the H. L. Hubbell company incorporate light fixtures, thus providing dual service as tables and attractive light gardens. Styles shown are, *top row, left to right:* Genoa; Independence, made of hard maple; and Tempo in butcher block hardwood. *Front row:* Milan, in ash and oak; Patriot, in maple; and Harmony. The Genoa and Harmony styles provide the most light with single or double 30-watt fixtures. Other styles come with single or double 15-watt fixtures, suitable for foliage plants or temporary display of flowering plants. (H. L. Hubbell, Inc., photo)

40 degrees. (Don't try this with gesneriads though; African-violets and *Episcias*, for example, do poorly with temperatures below 50°.) Leaving mature amaryllis and orchids outdoors in the fall provides both the long nights and cooler temperatures that these plants require for maximum bloom.

Nature's Days

Outside of the tropics, in the temperate zones where most of us live, day-length varies from about 9 to more than 15 hours according to the season. This variation, caused as the earth tilts in its orbit, provides both climatic changes and night-length cues for plant maturation. You can find out the day-length at any time of the year by consulting nautical or astronomical tables. The most available source is the classic *Farmer's Almanac*, published every year since 1792 and nationally available at most newsstands.

Important variations occur for plants that receive some natural daylight in addition to artifical light. In these situations you might wish to know in advance just when the longer days of spring begin or at what point in the fall nights will be twelve or more hours long.

Effects of Temperature

Some houseplants affected by night-length may also have blooming encouraged or retarded by temperature. *Primula malacoides*, normally a lovely winter-to-spring bloomer, will bud with long nights regardless of temperature; with short nights it blooms only when night temperatures are below 60°. With night temperatures above 60°, the short nights prevent flower formation.

This primrose is rewarding if you can provide the proper combination of temperature and light-hours. Other houseplants whose blooming is influenced by both temperature and light include some orchids and the Christmas cactus. Culture notes on these species are given in later chapters.

Energy-Saving Steps

With electric bills already high enough and our natural resources in need of conservation, we must try to save energy by following conservative procedures in the light garden:

1. Arrange dual lights wherever possible so that a fixture can offer two or more uses. For example, place a bookshelf fixture in a dark area where the spill light from it provides illumination where you need it in the room.

2. Set automatic timers to turn on lights at specific times each day and turn them off after the required light period. Tropical plants will grow and bloom with 12 hours of light, so if you wish to be frugal provide only 12 hours of artificial light per 24-hour period.

3. Capture all *natural* light possible. Locate light gardens near windows or glass-fronted doors. This lets plants receive the full-spectrum benefits from an hour or more of sun each day.

4. Use horticultural broad-spectrum lamps that provide the spectrum most utilized by plants rather than using inefficient incandescent bulbs.

5. Keep lamps clean and reflectors bright.

6. During the warm months, transfer some or all of your light-garden plants outdoors. They will make sturdy growth with nature's free light. The rain will cleanse foliage and flush accumulated chemical salts from the soil. You will be happier too, when the electric bill is lower.

7

The Environment: Air,
Humidity, Temperature

Light works with moisture in the air, temperature, and air circulation to foster sturdy growth. Under most conditions you can easily provide adequate humidity and air circulation. Fortunately the temperatures we enjoy indoors are satisfactory for hundreds of popular plants.

Temperature

The temperatures given in cultural directions are usually the minimum night temperatures for various species. Plants utilize stored food during dark hours. They grow most efficiently if temperatures during dark periods are 8° to 15°F lower than day-time (light-hour) highs.

I use two temperature ranges. One is the general range at which a given species grows into a sturdy specimen; a second is higher, reserved for starting seeds, propagating cuttings, encouraging rapid growth of select clones where adequate light is available. The temperature for propagation is a stimulating 8° to 10° higher than for standard growth, but still with a difference between light- and dark-hours.

Commercial growers employ temperature differences, depending upon what they want their plants to do. For example, the Rieger-Elatior begonias (see Chapter 15) are grown in the low 70's during light hours, 62–65°F at night, with 12-hour days for optimum flowering. For rapid development of young plants propagated from leaf or stem cuttings they are given 14-hour days in the high 70's and 72°–74° nights. The same range is good for most tropical houseplants. Of course, propagation can be managed at the average growing temperature for established plants, but germination of seeds and growth of cuttings are then slower.

Light and Temperature

Green plants are influenced by the relationship between light and temperature. As light intensity increases, temperature can rise to encourage rapid growth. However, as light levels decrease plants should receive lower temperatures, to keep their growth within bounds according to the available illumination.

A common problem with houseplants is high temperature and low light. Plants are sturdier under low light if temperatures remain on the low side of an acceptable range for each species. For example, if African-violets grow best with bright, diffuse light from two 40-watt fluorescent tubes placed 8 to 10 inches above foliage and with temperatures of 70°–75°F, they would not prosper if the light were reduced to a single 20-watt tube set 12 inches above them. However, if temperatures were reduced to 65°–70° and the light hours increased to 18 hours, the balance between temperature and light would produce better plants.

Fixture Heat

Active ballasts and lamps radiate heat, so turning on fixtures will raise day temperatures in their immediate vicinity.

If a multilevel light cart or several stacked bookshelves are involved, the higher shelves will be slightly warmer than the lower, due to heat from the fixtures below them. In custom-designed light gardens that have ballasts removed and placed away from fixtures, the heat will be less but the lamps will still raise the temperature a few degrees.

Enclosed Gardens

Plastic tents, glass fronts, Plexiglas panels, or similar barriers around a light garden will contain the heat. Since light-hour temperatures should be higher than dark-hour lows this is a useful effect. For cool growing plants, *Odontoglossum* orchids for example, venting may be required if temperatures get too high.

Small electric fans, sold in audio stores for cooling electronic equipment, are easy to install and quiet to run. Most of these minifans, lubricated for life, provide a simple means of forcing hot air out of the light-garden enclosure. To cool an area, locate the fan (blowing out) toward the top of a chamber or case. A small vent on the opposite side toward the bottom (just below pot levels) will draw in cool air.

Microclimates

You will find that your houseplants generally adapt to a temperature range of 60°–75°, the same temperatures preferred in our homes. However if you wish to grow high-altitude species or others that do best with nights down in the 50's, a microclimate can often be arranged. By placing your plants near a north window or locating the light garden on an unheated porch, in a cool basement, garage, or spare room, where heat can be cut down or a window opened, you can usually provide cool nights. This is true from fall into late spring in the temperate zone. Through the summer months even cool-growing orchids will tolerate higher temperatures if you maintain high humidity and vigorous air circulation. Air conditioning will not harm plants indoors but it does reduce humidity. In spacious light gardens and growing rooms a wet-pad evaporative cooler will keep summer temperatures under control. (These coolers are offered by the greenhouse supply firms listed in Chapter 21.)

Warm Microclimate

To produce a warm microclimate you have several options:

1. Locate the light garden near a basement heating unit.

2. Enclose the light area of shelf gardens with heavy plastic, fiberglass, or sparkling clear Plexiglas to retain normal fixture heat.

3. Grow warm-preference tropicals on top shelves of light carts or bookshelf gardens.

4. Install two 15- to 25-watt incandescent bulbs per 40-watt fluorescent fixture but keep foliage at least 4 to 6 inches away to avoid burn.

5. Place light fixtures in normally warmer areas, such as the kitchen.

Fortunately heat in most homes is around 70°–75° F by day and lower at night so no special temperature manipulation is required for the average light garden. Slightly higher or lower temperatures occur by virtue of location and fixture placement on tiered stands. Finding these microclimates with a maximum-minimum thermometer will usually save your

Maximum-minimum thermometers will help you discover microclimates within a growing area. Read high and low temperatures at the bottom of each indicator bar. Reset with small magnet provided.

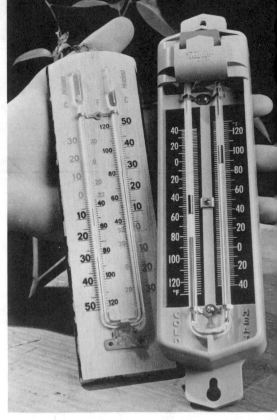

having to make alterations for occasional plants that have unusual temperature requirements.

Heat Cables

Inexpensive electric heat cables, offered in garden catalogs, will furnish extra bottom heat to speed propagation or give just enough warmth to protect cool-room light gardens during winter. The wire cables are spaced out under moist perlite, and the pots placed on the perlite. Built-in thermostats keep the cables from overheating.

Humidity

Moisture in the air is vital to houseplants. Only cactus and some other succulents can make optimum growth without at least 40 percent relative humidity. An average of 50 to 60

This plastic tent is made especially for tiered light-garden carts to conserve humidity around the plants inside. Keeping plants on moist gravel or coarse perlite will also supply humidity locally. (Tube Craft Inc. photo)

percent is satisfactory for tropicals under lights. Those species that need even higher humidity can be grown in terrariums or misted during the day.

Moisture Trays

Trays filled with moist perlite or gravel provide humidity immediately around your plants. Keep the water level below the top of your tray filling, then set pots on the moist material. If you want to keep roots from growing into the perlite or gravel, set pots on stiff wire grids placed above the water-filled trays or on individual saucers set in the moist material. Ridged "egg-crate" louvers and similar perforated plastic grates are also useful over trays of water, to keep pots from sitting in water and prevent roots from escaping. Growing plants above the filled trays helps avoid the inhibiting effects of dry air in light-garden areas.

Humidifiers

You will be healthier with 50 to 60 percent humidity in your living areas than the 15 to 30 percent humidity too often present in United States homes. With moderate humidity, less heat is required to make us comfortable, our skin does not crack, and paintings and wooden furniture last longer. A humidifier may be necessary unless your central heater has an adequate system. Most home-heating units have a water tray or wet pad that helps to moisten heated air. In apartments, dry basements, and attics supplementary humidifiers are often required to keep humidity at a 50 percent minimum.

Useful humidifiers include large-capacity, manually filled, electrically powered portable units and stationary foggers that are attached to a water line. The Herrmidifier is one such automatic device that puts out a fine fog by centrifugal force. A sensitive humistat controls the time when moisture is delivered, a feature found in the more sophisticated humidifiers.

The easiest way to increase humidity is with a hand-operated mister. Mist plants with warm water in the morning or at the start of light hours; be sure foliage is dry by night.

Air Circulation

Air, once moistened, should circulate around pots constantly. Moving air discourages fungus and brings a fresh supply of required gases to each leaf (carbon dioxide to be used during light hours, oxygen for respiration during dark hours). Small fans are a practical way to keep air in motion. A current that gently flutters foliage may blow directly at plants, but stronger airflows should be directed at a wall or up toward fixtures.

A fan blowing through a coarse-weave cloth or filter that is kept wet by having its base in water also helps to provide humidity. A similar result occurs if the fan blows at a small fountain or even a wet clay pot. Constantly moving air is of prime importance to orchids but all tropicals benefit from gently circulating air.

Fresh Air

New air from outside must also be brought into your light-garden area. In the warm months open a window nearby, but when it is cold outdoors avoid having a direct airflow hit indoor plants. Open a window in an adjoining room. By the time fresh air from outside reaches the houseplants it will be sufficiently tempered not to cause "bud blast" or other cold-draft problems.

Vacation Time

If you have to leave plants unattended for a week or so they will survive if you take some precautions. First, reduce their need for water by shortening the light-hours to eight to ten. The day before you leave, fill the moisture trays—but not so much that pots actually stand in water. Also water the soil in the pots.

The next day, when all foliage is dry but the soil moist, put thin plastic bags over each plant that you know usually dries out fast. This will not be necessary for geraniums, succulents, orchids, bulbs, bromeliads, and other species that have water storing organs, but the plastic protection will aid potbound coleus, begonias, gesneriads, and ferns. Plants in light-garden carts can be protected by hanging plastic around the whole cart, rather than over each plant.

If you will be gone more than ten days, arrange for someone to come in to water pots and refill moisture trays. The only plants that usually survive more than ten days neglect when in growth are succulents, bulbs, most orchids, and bromeliads. Other tropicals will do much better with some human attention.

Large foliage plants not under fluorescents can survive several weeks if you put them in tubs on top of soaking towels. On tiered light carts, separate the lower fixtures from the trays above by several inches to avoid rapid drying of the top trays due to heat from the ballasts below.

8
Containers and Methods of Watering

For maximum success fit the container size and material to the root system it will contain. Select containers first on the basis of what is best for each species, second for what looks nicest. If you do the reverse you may end up with an attractive collection of containers filled with rotted roots or stunted stems.

Pot Sizes and Styles

Unglazed clay pots, long the accepted container for houseplants, come in three basic styles: the standard type as deep as wide; the ¾-size pot, sometimes called an azalea pot, about a quarter wider than deep; and a shallow pot, sometimes called a bulb pan, just as wide as deep. Clay pots are measured across the top and vary slightly between potters, but the basic three styles and the width-to-depth ratios hold true. Plastic pots correspond to the clay-pot measurements but usually have additional drainage holes to compensate for the impermeability of most plastic containers.

Square Pots

Several companies make square plastic pots in useful sizes from 1½ to 8 inches, measured diagonally. These are excellent when you wish to conserve space since more of them can fit in a flat or under a fixture than an equal number of round pots. However once plants grow out beyond the rim this is not much of an advantage since pots will have to be spaced apart anyway.

How to Choose

Two major choices are based on horticultural requirements:
1. What *material* should the pot be made of?
2. What *size* should the pot be?

The material of a container is directly related to type of plant and conditions of growth. A major difference is between glazed or plastic containers, which do not transpire water and

Clay containers for indoor plants include an orchid pot at front left and a shallow bulb pan at rear right. Ornamental cork planter at back left is perfect for concealing clay pots while plants are on show; here *Begonia* 'Shirt Sleeves'.

thus dry out slowly, and the standard unglazed clay, which dries out fast.

In between are the foamy plastic containers, such as the Tufflite or Styrofoam pots. These are lightweight and do "breathe" like clay pots, although not as much.

Ornamental redwood planters are similar to the Styrofoam pots in that they do not dry out as fast as unglazed clay and do permit an exchange of air and some water evaporation through the sides.

Species that do best when dried out quickly after each soaking include most cactus and other succulents, and many epiphytic orchids. These thrive in unglazed clay containers. If your growing area is quite humid you might want to use standard clay containers for all plants, especially if you tend to overwater.

Plants that thrive with even moisture in the soil include seedlings, most foliage plants, many begonias, and gesneriads, including African-violets. If your growing conditions are dry or if you do not have the time to check plants every day, the slow-drying plastic pots will be more convenient.

The lightweight Styrofoam pots, available in white or terra-cotta color, are practical for the light garden. They are easily cleaned for reuse (I put mine in the dishwasher), and with adequate drainage in the bottom even succulents will grow well in Styrofoam pots.

Size

Overpotting almost always leads to rotted roots so it is better to use small- to medium-sized containers until roots fill the available soil, then transplant to slightly larger pots. Roots suffocate when excess soil remains soggy, as it tends to do when there are not enough roots to utilize the moisture.

Too drastic underpotting stunts plants and encourages roots to grow through the drainage holes, often filling the moisture trays. This is a problem when you wish to move a pot and find

Plastic containers for indoor plants can be clear, as for *Begonia pustulata* at left, and for the empty pot in center, white, or colored. At far right is a Tufflite Styrofoam pot with *Begonia* 'Switzerland'.

that the plant has more roots outside than inside the container. However in my light gardens some of the healthiest specimens have been those that escaped through drainage holes to grow extensive root systems in trays of moist perlite. Underpotting is less dangerous to plant health than overpotting.

Choose three-quarter-size azalea pots for shallow-rooted plants. African-violets, gloxinias, *Phalaenopsis* orchids, begonias (especially the creeping rhizomatous sorts)—all prosper in these wider-than-deep containers. Bulb pans are best for small spring bulbs, such as crocus, miniature narcissus, and squills. Azalea pots, with their added depth, are better suited to large tropical bulbs, such as amaryllis.

Succulents are suited to shallow pans, unglazed pots in any wider-than-deep shape, and to the three-quarter style pots. The wider-than-deep pots help stabilize top-heavy plants. For the same reason, I prefer heavy clay pots to lightweight plastic for plants that may require stakes or that tend to topple.

Succulents like this seedling cactus thrive in small shells if you tap a drainage hole in the bottom.

Self-Watering Containers

You can minimize watering by using containers that have a water reservoir sufficient for a week or more. Plastic self-watering pots come in several styles, the simplest of which is the pot with a fiber wick resting in a saucer of water under the pot. I have used this type of wick pot for years and find it an advantage for many terrestrial tropicals. The exceptions are tuberous or bulbous species and those plants that do best with complete dryness between watering such as succulents or epiphytics.

In Park's "Easy Does It" self-watering pot the stopper must be seated airtight.

A sophisticated version of the self-watering pot is the reservoir wall container that is actually a double pot with a hollow space to hold water, poured in through a small top hole. If the stopper is a hundred percent tight, the idea works but should the slightest bit of air get through around the cork, the water will keep rising through the soil until the inner soil-filled pot has the same water-level as the outer reservoir, thus drowning the roots.

Easy Wicking

To make your own self-watering containers, buy fiberglass rope or woven wick material, cut off a 2 to 3-inch wick, and push it up the drainage hole of an already planted pot. Set the pot on a stiff wire grid or layer of large stones with the wick end dangling in water. As the soil begins to dry, water will be drawn up the wick and help to keep the roots moist. Some African-violet growers keep the wick ends constantly in water, but I prefer to let a day or two pass before refilling the water reservoir. If you are using wicks when you are repotting, extend the wick about 1 inch into the soil and 2 inches out of the drainage hole.

Undrained Containers

Containers without any drainage holes are very difficult to use because watering is such a problem. There is no easy way to get rid of mineral salts that gradually accumulate in the soil and roots run high risk of rotting. Rather than use undrained containers as the original planter, I suggest growing

Sedum rubrotinctum from Guatemala thrives in a well-drained, partially glazed clay pot.

houseplants in fully drained pots. Then, if you wish to have a container for display, put the growth pot inside of an undrained display pot. You can adjust the height of plants inside decorative outer containers by placing under them gravel, a small upturned pot, or even an inverted pot saucer or two.

Terrariums

Nearly closed, clear containers of glass or plastic get much too hot if kept in sunlight, but the cool rays of fluorescents provide light for growing without dangerously high heat. After years of growing delicate tropicals under varied conditions, I consider fluorescent light the best illumination for terrariums.

This terrarium requires little water and receives diffuse light from fluorescents overhead. The cover is a plastic prismatic panel.

Some fixtures, such as those with circline growth lamps, are well suited to glass-bowl or low circular plastic terrariums. The self-supporting 20- or 40-watt fixtures, holding two lamps each, are effective above terrariums planted in oblong glass containers such as fish tanks.

Terrariums placed on coffee tables or elsewhere in living areas will benefit from incandescent reading lights, but keep the bulbs at least six inches away to prevent high temperatures inside the terrarium.

Watering

Only terrariums with cacti and other drought-resistant succulents can endure low humidity, long periods of no water, and strong sun. Most terrariums are planted with forest-floor species that thrive with high humidity and diffuse light. These must be kept evenly moist. Modern terrariums are not completely closed but allow some ventilation. Slight condensation should appear on the top and sides of an adequately moist terrarium. This will be most evident when the outside temperature changes in morning or late afternoon.

If no interior condensation appears, the terrarium requires water. I like to use rain water or spring water to avoid the chemical salts found in many water supplies. A turkey baster is good for watering terrariums. For full details on creating and caring for terrariums see my *The Complete Book of Terrariums* (New York: Hawthorn Books, Inc., 1974), which is devoted to this fascinating way to grow plants.

Guide to Watering

Apply room-temperature water to avoid the shock and foliage spotting that sometimes results from cold water. If your local supply is heavily chlorinated, draw water a day or two in advance and let it stand in an open container so the

Mexican animalito pots are amusing but require careful watering since they have no drainage hole.

chlorine gas can escape. Fortunately, over most of the country tap water may be used just as it runs.

Plants under lights require watering more often than the same species in a greenhouse or at a window. Succulents still do best drying out a little between watering. African-violets thrive with an evenly moist soil, and under constant bright light they often require more water than at windows. Water can be applied from above, with care to keep it off the foliage, or from below.

Bottom-Watering

Under lights, plants usually need so much water that they wilt if you cannot attend to them at least every other day. One safeguard is bottom watering. A fiberglass wick inserted through the drainage hole lets moisture travel into the root area when the wick end is set in water.

Another system is to let wicks dangle down through wood or wire slats into trays filled with water that furnishes some local

Anthurium polyschistum (top) and *Gynura aurantiaca* are two of the many foliage species that will live for months in a weak fertilizer solution or even in plain water.

humidity. I have had plants create their own wicks when roots grow into the water pans. This often happens with epiphytic orchids with their traditionally wandering roots. Most of their roots are in airy potting mixes of bark or tree fern, but the few roots that grow into the water help the plant maintain a good moisture balance.

When terrestrial plants grow in pots above trays of moist perlite or gravel, roots grow out of the drainage holes into the moist material below. Fertilizer salts also wash down through the pots into the perlite or gravel so roots that escape have a hydroponic environment in which to prosper. After a month plants may have more roots outside the pots than in.

This is no problem but a useful way for plants to get water from below and still keep the foliage dry, which is important with some gesneriads and the Rieger begonias. Plants set directly on a moist material can go longer without watering than plants totally confined in their containers. Always make sure pots do not stand in water longer than an hour after watering.

Should you have to move or repot a plant that has extensive roots outside a pot, break the pot open or crack the sides in order to save the roots. Or prune back the roots with sharp scissors, then cut off a corresponding amount of top growth. Few plants can have half their root system removed without losing some top growth too, so it is best to do all the surgery at one time. Remember that top cuttings from numerous houseplants are excellent for propagation. (See Chaper 19.)

Standard Top-Watering

Top-watering has one main advantage: you control how much water goes into the soil. The flow carries mineral accumulations downward and, with adequate watering, eventually out the drainage hole. At least every third or fourth watering, water should pour out of drainage holes. Some plants, such as the epiphytic orchids, should be watered liberally every time. Plants given plastic-coated slow-release fertilizers must also be flooded from above so that the water can draw out the fertilizer in minute quantities.

Bottom drainage material—gravel, crocks, pebbles—will provide about one half to one inch of soil-free space, a beneficial protection for pots on moist material or in saucers. Without drainage material inside the pots roots might stand in water too long.

For Healthy Roots

The techniques that assure healthy roots while still permitting you to soak the plants are:

1. Adequate drainage material inside the pots.
2. Sufficient depth to the moist material in trays on which pots rest. Trays should contain at least 1 inch of gravel or 1 inch of gravel below a half-inch layer of coarse perlite.

A substitute to having pots touch moist material in a tray is to sit pots on wire grids or wood slats above trays of water. In all cases the goal is to give you freedom to water each pot completely without having to worry that accumulations of water will rot the roots.

I found these clumps of *Cyperus alternifolius* in a sunny Kenyan swamp. Such bog plants thrive when kept quite moist, but most houseplants should not set in water.

Watering Aids

Various aids are helpful in keeping water off foliage and fixtures. A device I bought from the Tube Craft company works like a siphon. A container of water, like a large plastic jug, is placed higher than the plants. The watering wand has a long plastic tube with a weight on one end which sinks into the jug or water bucket. On the other end is a thin, light-weight squeeze-to-water handle and an 18-inch aluminum wand that insures accuracy. So long as the water supply is higher than the pots, waterflow works perfectly.

Hydrogel Soil Amendment

A new soil amendment called Viterra (Union Carbide Corporation) is useful in reducing the effects of water stress or excessive drying of ornamental plants. Viterra is a granular hydrogel made from polymeric material which absorbs water by swelling into tiny lumps of gelled liquid. The material has been used for several years by commercial growers to reduce the need for frequent watering of potted plants and to avoid damage to plants due to wilting.

Viterra hydrogel is offered in the Burpee Seed Co. catalog for home use. Complete directions are supplied on the packs of Viterra. For indoor plants sprinkle 5.4 oz. (the whole retail size pack) on top of ½ bushel (16 quarts) of your soil mix. Thoroughly mix the hydrogel powder with the soil ingredients. This amendment is compatible with all of the soil mixtures I list in Chapter 9, including the soil-free peatmoss-perlite formulas. The one caution mentioned by the manufacturers of Viterra is *not* to use a Dexon fungicide drench on plants which have Viterra in the mix. According to tests all other commonly used chemicals and fungicides are compatible with Viterra. Only the Dexon fungicide caused Viterra to loose its water-holding ability.

9

Potting Mixes and Fertilizers

Soil gives physical support to roots and with most mixes also provides the nutrients required for sturdy growth. Recently many commercial growers have turned to the soilfree mixes, first developed by agricultural researchers and made famous by Cornell University. Several brands are now found in garden stores for home use. Jiffy Mix, Sure-Fire Potting Mix, and Kys Mix are variations of the perlite, peatmoss, vermiculite formulas. I like the peatlite mixes but add 15 to 25 percent of soil for weight and to provide basic nutrients for plants under lights.

Basic Mix

In my light gardens and greenhouses hundreds of plants thrive in the basic mix I describe later in this chapter. Exceptions are epiphytic orchids and bromeliads which, in nature, live perched on trees. These epiphytes must have a well-aerated medium so I pot them in mixes of tree fern, tree bark (fir and redwood), and coarse perlite (Sponge Rok). You can make such mixtures or purchase orchid-potting composts from some of the firms listed in Chapter 21.

Soil additives customize potting mixes. Top row, all-purpose houseplant soil and dolomite limestone powder. Second row left to right, perlite, sphagnum peatmoss, and unmilled sphagnum moss. Bottom row left to right, coarse sand, vermiculite, and hardwood charcoal chunks for the drainage layer.

Ingredients

In addition to good garden soil (loam), what are the best ingredients for houseplant mixes?

Bark Chips. The most-used are fir and redwood, both popular for orchid mixes, available in large, medium, and small chunks, and as the fuzzy-substanced bark wool. The small grade lightens soil for semi-epiphytic gesneriads and cactus. Complete mixes for orchids use bark combined with coarse perlite, and sometimes tree-fern or chopped sphagnum moss. Soil and sphagnum peatmoss are added for terrestrial orchids such as *Paphiopedilum*.

Dolomite Limestone Powder. This is a long-lasting form of limestone that contains considerable magnesium. Useful to balance acid in peatmoss but not always required.

Leafmold. Pasteurized oakleaf mold, offered in bags by some suppliers, is a useful form of humus for mixing with commercial potting soils.

Loam. Good garden soil or loam is a combination of clay, sand, and decayed organic matter or humus. Pasteurized soil sold in plastic bags is a safe and convenient substitute for garden soil. Unpasteurized soil from outdoors usually contains pests and weed seeds that cause problems in the light garden.

Peatmoss. This is partially decayed bog plants, usually sphagnum moss, with slight nutritional value. Coarse sphagnum peatmoss is a primary ingredient in most houseplant mixes and the basis for modern soilfree formulas. Much finer, almost soil-like, is black peat, such as Baccto Peat. This kind of peatmoss does not lighten soil as well as the coarser sphagnum peatmoss, but it is useful in mixes for terrestrial plants such as African-violets.

Perlite. This white volcanic rock, offered in several grades from extra coarse Sponge Roc to an almost dustlike fine grind, is popular for germinating small seeds. By holding air and water, the perlite encourages vigorous root growth, helps prevent soil compaction. Perlite is useful in mixes for all houseplants, but it is much lighter than sand. For top-heavy species and cactus, sand is also used or substituted for perlite to give weight. Combine medium-grind perlite half-and-half with milled sphagnum moss for an excellent propagating and seed-starting mix.

Sand. This is the universal ingredient in traditional potting mixes. The sand to use is medium-to-coarse builder's sand. Avoid beach sand and ultra-fine ornamental sands. Clean pasteurized coarse sand suitable for houseplant soils is sold in bags for children's play areas. Sakrette is one nationally available brand. Use sand to add weight for tall plants and to improve drainage.

Sphagnum Moss. Sphagnum grows in bogs and sometimes in wet cloud forests. In the unprocessed form it comes as long golden-brown strands, usually dry in bales. For seed starting the dry strands are crushed through a fine sieve to produce milled sphagnum, a fluffy sweet-smelling substance. Sphagnum has antibacterial properties that make it useful for seed sowing. The unmilled strands are good as is or chopped in mixes for orchids. I also use unmilled sphagnum for some bulbs and various tropicals that need special care. For example, a plant that is subject to root rot in soil may thrive when tightly potted in unmilled sphagnum. You can obtain natural or milled sphagnum from several garden firms listed in Chapter 21.

Vermiculite. Mica is heated and expanded to produce vermiculite, a golden, somewhat shiny, soft mineral that can retain a quantity of water in its layers. Horticultural grades of vermiculite come in fine and medium-sized pellets, offered in various size bags. The fine grade has limited value for starting small seeds; the medium grade vermiculite is widely used in soil mixes, for seed starting and for rooting cuttings.

Since vermiculite has many thin layers in each grain, it holds moisture and absorbs fertilizer salts, a buffering action favorable to root growth, but if too much vermiculite is used with soil roots may die from lack of oxygen. If you tend to overwater plants, use perlite in your propagating mixes instead of vermiculite. Add only recommended amounts of vermiculite in potting mixes unless you want a soil that stays wet. Vermiculite gets soft and slippery when crushed so perlite or gravel is preferable for filling moisture trays. The best use of vermiculite is in potting mixes where it is combined with perlite, sphagnum peatmoss, and loam.

Basic Soil Mixture

1 quart commercial pasteurized houseplant soil (or pasteurized garden loam)

3 quarts coarse perlite (white volcanic rock in granular form)

6 quarts dry or just-moist sphagnum peatmoss (medium to coarse)

4–6 tablespoons powdered dolomite limestone (omit for plants that prefer very acid soil, i.e., azaleas, gardenias, citrus) Combine the ingredients thoroughly in a big, clean tub, wheelbarrow, or plastic refuse container. Or put the ingredients in a heavy plastic bag, tie the top, and mix by kneading the bag. Do not moisten until just before using.

This mixture will support most begonias, gesneriads, and other tropicals. It may be modified according to the specific requirements of an individual species. For example:

To hold moisture longer in the soil, add 1 quart vermiculite (Terra-lite or similar medium-grade).

To add weight for top-heavy plants, add 1 quart sand or use all sand rather than perlite.

For semi-epiphytic plants or others that require very airy compost, add 2 quarts fine- to medium-grade fir or redwood bark.

For plants, such as geraniums, that do well in heavier mixes; add 2 to 3 quarts soil.

Fertilizers

With this basic soil mixture and its variations, fertilizer should be applied after the first few weeks. There is so little soil in the formula that you can actually control plant growth according to how you fertilize. For plants grown entirely under fluorescent lights, apply fertilizer in quarter to half

First step in repotting is to invert a plant with your fingers placed around the base and over the soil. Tap the edge of the pot and the root ball will fall out.

Set the old pot in the partially filled new container; then fill in soil around the smaller pot. Remove the old pot and the resulting cavity will be the same size as the root ball to be set inside.

strength (as listed on the package) at every watering. Choose a formula in keeping with the species, as outlined later in this chapter. Plants that receive only *some* supplemental light from fluorescents or incandescents will not need so much fertilizer due to weather variations that affect the amount of light, especially during the winter. Therefore fertilize them every third watering.

Water-soluble Fertilizers

Use water-soluble houseplant fertilizers that dissolve quickly in lukewarm water, as Hyponex, Miracle-Gro, and Peters. Every few weeks omit fertilizer and apply fresh water freely to flush away fertilizer salts that tend to burn roots if the buildup is too great. To be sure plants receive all the necessary trace elements, I often alternate organic fish emulsion formulas with water-soluble chemical types.

Fertilizers sold in the United States must show content and percentage of active ingredients on each package. The three major nutrients—nitrogen, phosphorus, and potassium (potash)—are always listed in the same order. Each contributes a different value to a growing plant and, along with trace elements in minute quantities, all are required for normal development.

Single Serving

With one application of a balanced fertilizer you are supplying nitrogen to promote foliage growth and production of new tissues, phosphorus to aid cell formation, especially in roots and reproductive cells, and finally potassium. The potassium (potash) encourages strong stem growth and maturation for flowering and seed development.

Popular fertilizers also contain trace elements, such as calcium, copper, iron, sulfur, and zinc. To be sure your plants receive all necessary elements, alternate two or three brands and from time to time apply an organic formula.

Seaweed

For most of my life I have lived by the sea where it was our custom to harvest seaweed for a natural garden mulch and fertilizer. Blueberries, bulbs, roses, all have flowers of deeper color and sturdier stems when they are mulched with seaweed, but only recently has seaweed been available in a portable, liquefied form for houseplant use.

My plants now receive the trace elements and associated nutrients of seaweed when I fertilize them with the liquefied material, sometimes mixed with a chemical fertilizer just before I apply the solution. Several brands of seaweed fertilizer are available, and I find them acceptable for tropicals in the light garden, when mixed according to directions or in slightly weaker dilutions.

Constant Application

A weak feeding with *every* watering is suitable where plants receive 12 or more hours of light per 24-hour period. Since there are no cloudy days in a light garden, plants grow at an even rate, faster than the same species at a window or in a greenhouse. Using weak fertilizer at every watering provides a constant supply of nutrients, insures sturdy deficiency-free growth.

For example, I often use Miracle-Gro or Peters 18–18–18, a quarter teaspoon per gallon, on begonias, gesneriads, ferns, orchids in active growth, and on other tropicals in my light-garden areas. Rather than fertilize once a month with full-strength solutions, I find the plants do better with constant weak applications. In any case, fertilizer is used to supply nutrients *only* when other growth requirements are met. Fertilizer will not make up for inadequate light, low humidity, or other inhospitable factors.

Slow-release fertilizer Osmocote 14–14–14 at top; bottom left Precise African-violet 8–11–5; at right is green colored Precise 12–6–6 foliage and a general-use formula.

Slow-Release Products

Another method of constant application involves slow-release, plastic-coated pellets. Osmocote, Poracel, and 3–M Precise are of this kind, the chemicals locked in a permeable plastic coat. Every time water is applied, a small quantity of fertilizer is released from the plastic ball. With the slow-release granules it is important to water freely so as to release the fertilizer and also to prevent root burn. I find the slow releases convenient for any plant that grows continuously under lights. One application furnishes nutrients for three to four months. I use these fertilizers on my Rieger begonias, orchids, and anthuriums. The 3–M Precise African-violet granules are suitable for all gesneriads.

Formulas

Slow-release formulas should be suited to the species being grown, as are the water-soluble chemical formulas. Foliage plants generally do best with fertilizers somewhat high in nitrogen since this nutrient encourages leafy growth. Flowering plants bloom better with a balanced fertilizer or one high in phosphorus and potassium (potash), which promote good stem growth and budding.

Suitable ratios found in houseplant fertilizers are 15–30–15 of Peters House Plant Special and Stern's Miracle-Gro, two widely used water-soluble formulas. Hyponex 7–6–19 and Peters African-violet fertilizer 12–36–14 are lower in nitrogen, higher in other elements that encourage bloom. Fish emulsions, chemical fertilizers, such as Peters 21–7–7 and Rapid-gro 23–19–17, all have more nitrogen in proportion to phosphorus and potassium, and so promote growth.

Good slow-release fertilizers include 3–M Precise African-violet food 8–11–5 and Osmocote 14–14–14. A similar water-soluble formula is Peters 20–19–18 designed for plants in soilfree mixes or mixes with high proportions of perlite, peatmoss, and vermiculite. With any of these products, apply slightly weaker than directed on the package as insurance against overfertilization which damages roots.

Compressed Fertilizers

Another gradual-release type is the fertilizer pellet, a compressed nutrient powder that is pushed into the soil. The pellets do not require much water to make them work, compared with plastic-coated slow-release types, and they are hidden. I prefer the granules, which stay on the soil surface, so I can see when they are used up. However, if you don't like the granules, then use the compressed tablets.

Tropicals grow so quickly under adequate fluorescent light that mineral deficiencies show up more often than in window plants. A symptom in azaleas, anthuriums, citrus shrubs,

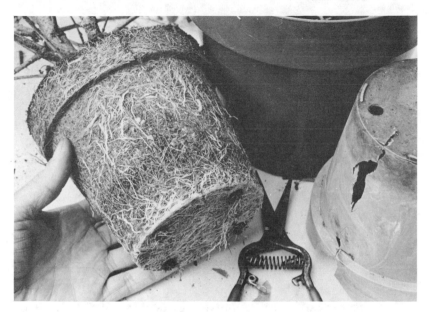

When roots fill the container, plants require water more often. After several months a plant will usually need repotting as with this potbound gardenia.

Potting epiphytic orchids requires some special materials if roots are to remain healthy. At top is a burner to flame sterilize cutting tools, a precaution against spreading disease from clone to clone; a chunk of tree-fern, a potting stick, unmilled sphagnum moss for holding additional moisture around fine-rooted orchids, and hardwood charcoal. At lower right, is chopped tree-fern; in center, bark chips and white coarse perlite. A waterproof marker and plastic labels help keep plant names straight.

gardenias, and some tropical bulbs is iron chlorosis, which is comparable to iron-deficiency anemia in humans. Foliage turns light green, then yellow. The cure is to supply extra iron. Spray foliage weekly with soluble fertilizer that contains iron chelates, such as Stern's Miracid. Also water the soil with a solution of horticultural iron such as Green Garde (Encap Products Co.) micronized iron. Green Garde powder may also be sprinkled on top of the soil or incorporated into soil ingredients when you are mixing potting soil. Iron chelate Sequestrene (Geigy Chemical Co.) is another good product.

Acid-Alkaline Balance

Most houseplants thrive in the Basic Soil Mix described earlier without attention to the acid-alkaline condition or pH. Commercial pasteurized potting soils are balanced to the acidity preferred by popular indoor plants. However, soils that include peatmoss, leafmold, or bark chips become progressively acid with the decomposition of these organic ingredients.

If a healthy plant, established for a year or more, shows abnormally slow growth, regardless of favorable environmental conditions, it may be starved for nutrients in a soil that has become too acid. The cure is to sprinkle dolomite limestone (1 teaspoon per 3- to 4-inch pot) over the soil. With each top watering the soil will become slightly less acid.

Testing

Usually you will have success with houseplants without having to test for pH values. However, you can determine the acid-alkaline balance of your potting soil by sending a sample to your county agricultural agent. You can also try a home test with a Sudbury or other kit, or use the inexpensive pH-testing tapes that change color according to the acidity of the soil when it is in solution.

PART II

PLANTS TO GROW

In this section each popular plant group has been given a separate chapter. Then interesting species in numerous genera from many parts of the world are discussed, such as foliage plants in Chapter 14, or certain flowering treasures in Chapter 17. Miniature roses and bulbs to grow under lights are included.

For quick reference I have recommended an average distance between lamps and each plant, for example, *Caladium:* 4"-10". Closer settings promote compact growth, longer ones allow space for flowers, particularly under broad-spectrum lamps.

The scientific names used in this book are the basis of order in horticulture, but I have also included accepted popular names whenever possible.

10
Gesneriads, Champions Under Lights

The champion houseplants under lights have got to be gesneriads. Thanks to the most popular member, the African-violet, no other plant family has achieved so wide and complete a popularity with thousands of indoor light gardeners around the world. Of course, the gesneriads themselves have much to offer when the bright days they receive under fluorescent lamps produce a constant succession of flowers. More flower show prizes go to African-violets grown under lights than to similar plants from bright windows or greenhouses.

Even Illumination

A major charm of African-violets (*Saintpaulia* hybrids), gloxinias (*Sinningia* hybrids), and related gesneriads is their fuzzy foliage arranged in symmetrical rosettes. By growing gesneriads under fluorescent lamps it is easy to obtain delightfully full plants with abundant flowers and attractive foliage. No turning is required to keep growth even, and fluorescent light will not burn leaves the way hot sun can.

African-violets (*Saintpaulia* hybrids) come in an extraordinary variety of colors and forms. New hybrids are introduced every year, many are similar. Select your favorites from color-illustrated catalogues or at flower shows.

Gesneriads would not be so popular if they were not so adaptable. African-violets thrive with the 65° to 75° temperatures we have in our homes. Many other striking gesneriads, including new dwarf strains of *Streptocarpus* (cape-primrose) and tiny *Sinningia* hybrids, also thrive within this temperature range. Hybridists have further increased adaptability through selection of breeding stock. Now the hybrids offered in specialists' catalogues are not only more compact, longer lasting, and more colorful, but usually they are also more forgiving when confronted with slightly warmer or cooler temperatures than those required by the original species.

Growth Styles

Gesneriads are classified according to flower form and plant habit. The main divisions are:

Fibrous-rooted genera, including African-violets derived from the East African *Saintpaulia* species; *Aeschynanthus*, known as the Lipstick Vines; and *Episcia* cultivars, creeping forest-floor plants from South America.

Tuberous-rooted genera, including the florists' large gloxinias, *Sinningia speciosa* hybrids, (formally called *Rechsteineria*), and such new miniature sinningias as 'Bright Eyes' and 'Dollbaby', both perfect for terrariums.

Rhizome-rooted genera include those that form scaley rhizomes underground, such as *Achimenes* and *Smithiantha*, the Temple Bells.

Culture Basics

The fibrous-rooted gesneriads (*Saintpaulia, Streptocarpus, Episcia,* etc.) must always be kept moist because they have no underground storage organs. Species with tubers or rhizomes have a means of storing water for periods of drought; in fact, they require a dry rest in captivity.

Gloxinias may stay dormant for six to ten weeks, but the scaley rhizomes of kohlerias or the tubers of sinningias may resprout as soon as older growth has bloomed and died back. Fibrous-rooted genera are active throughout the year, but tuberous and rhizomatous kinds go dormant from time to time.

Potting, Soil, Watering

So many of the original species live in rich humus on the jungle floor (*Episcia*), in tree crotches with rotting leaves around the roots (*Aeschynanthus, Columnea*), or in pockets of humus among rocks (*Achimenes, Streptocarpus*), that shallow pots are best. Gesneriads develop fibrous roots close to the soil surface so containers wider than deep are suitable. I have studied such species as the kohlerias, that sometimes live in average soil, but I note that it is always well drained, often sandy, never soggy.

Soil for gesneriads should be fluffy and well drained but still capable of retaining an even amount of moisture. Gesneriads thrive in the basic mix given in Chapter 9. They also grow well in Black Magic mix, or the mixtures offered by professional gesneriad growers, such as the G-B-S mix of Kartuz Greenhouses or variations of soilfree mixtures based on sphagnum peatmoss and perlite. Plants in such soils require a constant supply of nutrients from water-soluble fertilizers.

Draw water a day before so it will be at room temperature, or take care to mix tap water so that it is lukewarm. Cold water shocks roots, spots foliage. I water most of my gesneriads from above, pouring the water gently on top of the soil; many growers have success with wick pots. Whatever system you use, avoid a soggy soil. Dormant tuberous and rhizomatous gesneriads, with no top growth, require just enough moisture to keep them from shriveling. They are safe in their original pots and soil for resting periods, so long as the soil does not become dust-dry.

Light Hours and Intensity

An average of 14 hours of light per 24-hour period will provide gesneriads with sufficient energy for healthy growth. Gardeners around the country and several research projects on gloxinias and African-violets confirm that these plants also bloom freely with such long days. Up to 18 hours per day is acceptable, especially for seedlings that you wish to see bloom soon. You will have excellent African-violets, episcias, streptocarpus, columneas, and most other genera with 14 to 16 light-hours per 24-hour period. Gesneriads are mainly indeterminate or day-neutral species.

Provide medium-to-strong light from at least two fluorescent tubes for gloxinias and streptocarpus. African-violets and episcias need less light, but all are easy to judge from leaf color and shape. African-violets that are receiving too strong light will be yellowish and quite compact, sometimes with twisted leaves or abnormally close foliage.

When light intensity is right, leaf color will be medium green or darker, if that is natural, as in some saintpaulias or smithianthas with maroon foliage. If leaf stems are overlong, or plants fail to bloom after several months of growth, then the light is insufficient; move plants closer to the lamps, or if the ends are dark change the lamps for new tubes. For the first 100 to 150 hours the lamps burn, keep African-violets 10 to 12 inches away to avoid yellow or contorted new leaves.

Recent experiments show improved flowering when standard Gro-Lux tubes (those with a rosy glow) are combined with Wide-Spectrum Gro-Lux, one to one. Many growers obtain adequate bloom when Cool White and Warm White tubes supplement diffuse sunlight. In my own collection gesneriads thrive with broad-spectrum lamps, such as Agro-Lites and Wide-Spectrum Gro-Lux. Some African-violets bloom well with the Cool White-Warm White combination, especially when plants also receive an hour or two of early morning sun. Gesneriads are adaptable enough to bloom under various kinds of fluorescent lamps if plants are given adequate light intensity, 50 percent humidity, and temperatures of 65° to 75°.

Some Delightful Gesneriads

Achimenes. (3″–6″)* Plant five or six of the peanut-sized rhizomes in each shallow 6-inch pot. Keep evenly moist throughout the growing season. Most cultivars trail although some, such as 'Crimson Beauty' and 'Tarantella' (big pink) can be formed into low mounds by several early pinchings. The 1/2 inch petunia-shaped flowers appear over several months, then plants go dormant for 2–3 months. Best for bloom summer into fall. Provide 16-hour light periods for flowers.

* The measurement indicates the distance the plant is to be placed from the lamp.

Achimenes 'Menuett', deep pink.

Aeschynanthus. (4″–10″) The lipstick vines get their common name from bright scarlet tubular flowers. Grow plants with warm 65°–70° nights, train on stakes or pinch to keep bushy. They will also grow draped over a moist pole of tree fern or a "log" of unmilled sphagnum, as sometimes used for trailing philodendrons. 'Black Pagoda' is an odd green and maroon flowered hybrid with lovely mottled leaves. *A.obconicus* has lasting red flowers, nearly oval foliage. Similar in bloom are *A.lobbianus*, *A.parvifolius*, and *A.pulcher*, the classic lipstick vines with trailing stems, glossy pointed foliage, and clusters of brilliant red flowers. *A.micranthus* (red flowers) and *A.tricolor* (red and yellow with purple stripes) are compact dwarfs, good under light.

Boea hygroscopica. (6″–10″) Plant this low, fibrous-rooted rosette of fuzzy green in a terrarium for lush growth. Flowers are blue marked yellow inside.

118

Chirita sinensis. (6″–10″) Select this fibrous-rooted low species for silver patterned foliage, occasional light lavender flowers. Provide a warm, humid atmosphere for best foliage, but this is adaptable and will also do well beside African-violets.

Columnea. (4″–10″) Although most columneas are vines, they will thrive under light and bloom freely when provided with enough intensity. Pinch tips to keep plants bushy. Columneas are fibrous-rooted and must be kept evenly moist. They do best in rather small pots since the species frequently live as epiphytes on moss-covered limbs. Select compact hybrids with everblooming tendencies for light gardens, like 'Red Spur', 'Yellow Hammer', and the compact everblooming rose-red 'Mary Ann', a new Kartuz hybrid. Columneas produce 1-3 inch flowers over a period of months, and pollinated flowers are followed by ornamental berries. Modern hybrids do well with 60°–65° nights but accept temperatures into the mid 50's.

Episcia. (6″–10″) The episcias are fibrous-rooted trailers grown for metallic-toned and delicately veined foliage.

Episcia 'Cygnet', white with purple dots.

They succeed with warm humid conditions (65°–70° nights). Although they do not require as much light as African-violets, they thrive alongside their popular relatives in a light garden. Some of my favorites are 'Cygnet' with green foliage and unique fringed white flowers with purple spots, and 'Acajou', a cultivar of *E.cupreata*, with silver leaves and bright red flowers. All kinds are easily propagated from runners or tip cuttings.

Gesneria. (4"–6") Tiny, 1"–2" tall *G.cuneifolia* variant *quebradillas* has shiny, dark green leaves and tubular 1" orange flowers constantly when under lights. This fibrous-rooted miniature thrives in a terrarium. 'Lemon Drop' is a Kartuz selection with yellow flowers.

x Gloxinera. See *Sinningia*.

Gloxinia. See *Sinningia*.

Hypocyrta. See *Nematanthus*.

Koellikeria. (4"–6") These have miniature 2–4 inch rosettes of silver-speckled foliage growing from scaly rhizomes; plants are seldom dormant. Flowers, produced on upright spikes, are white with red markings. A good terrarium plant.

Kohleria. (4"–6") This genus produces upright 12- to 20-inch stems, heavily covered with fuzzy leaves, red margined in *K.eriantha*. Flowers are 1 to 2 inches long, opening in clusters. Colors range from pinks to red and yellow, often with spots in contrasting tones. Pot one to three rhizomes per 4-inch pot, placing rhizomes horizontally. Cover with 1 inch of soil and keep lightly moist until sprouts appear, then increase watering. For sturdy growth keep foliage close to lamps as sprouts first appear, then increase distance for maturation and flowers. 'Connecticut Belle' and 'Princess' are two excellent, compact, pink-flowered modern hybrids. For large red flowers grow K. 'Longwood'. In fall and winter give six weeks of 13–14-hour nights to nearly mature plants of *K.digitaliflora*, *K.eriantha*, and any others that seem reluctant to bloom with shorter nights.

Nematanthus. (4″–6″) For years most *Nematanthus* were known as *Hypocyrta* species, but recently the names were changed by taxonomists. No matter what label, you will enjoy growing some of these compact, glossy-leaved, fibrous-rooted gems under lights. The newer hybrids, created mainly by William Saylor, combine the attractive characteristics of different species. For example, *N.* 'Cheerio' (*N.gregarius* x *N.wettsteinii*) is a free-flowering, compact trailer with waxy deep-green foliage and orange pouch-shaped flowers. A fine species is *N.wettsteinii* which has red-and-yellow flowers on trailing stems, succulent, shiny dark green leaves. Of different habit, more open, with 10–15-inch stems, is the hybrid *N.* 'Black Magic', valuable for the unusual dark purple leaves and orange flowers marked pink produced on short dangling stems. Pinch to keep compact, root stem-tips for propagation.

Rechsteineria. See *Sinningia*.

Saintpaulia. (4″–8″) African-violets are one of the tropicals that actually do better under fluorescent lights than in a greenhouse. You can have a constant succession of flowers in a wide range of colors and shapes by growing African-violets and nothing else. Even though the saintpulia hybrids are varied, they look even nicer with

Miniature African-violets 'Tiny Blue' (left) and 'Snow In'.

such compatible companions as aeschynanthus, begonias, and some of the smaller orchids. African-violets have shallow fibrous roots. They do best in bulb pans, tubs, or azalea-type pots. Plastic containers prevent the leaf burn associated with clay containers, which accumulate salts and stay moist along the top rim.

Varieties with plain green foliage need less light than those with bronze or red-tinted leaves. Place tinted leaf sorts toward the center of fixtures; the plants with light-colored green leaves toward the ends or edges. Minimum nights 65°–68° are suitable. Maintain evenly moist soil but do not let pots stand in water for more than 1/2 hour after watering. Soggy soil rots roots.

After a year or so even miniature African-violets form long stems bare of lower leaves. You can shorten plants and improve flowering by repotting in fresh soil. Knock the plant out of its pot, trim off the lower row or two of leaves flush with the stem, cut away about one third of the old roots, and repot 1 inch deeper into a relatively small pot. Saintpaulias thrive in containers where roots can fill the soil. Too much soil leads to rot.

My African-violets provide a parade of flowers, but not on every plant. Each one blooms for a month or more, then usually rests a few weeks before producing the next flush of flowers. The hybrids I have grow well under various fluorescents, even with the Cool White/Warm White one:one combination. However, the most consistent bloom, over long periods, occurs under Wide-Spectrum Gro-Lux.

So many people are hybridizing saintpaulias that you may find it hard to select varieties from the extensive catalogue listings. Many cultivars are similar, even though they have different names. Seeing the plants in color photos or at a flower show is the best way to choose. Some outstanding hybrids that will be around for many years include the Rhapsodie cultivars, bred for abundant flowers and an adaptable habit. They come in many colors with both single- and double-flower forms.

Other exciting trends in new African-violets are the miniature trailers introduced by hybridizer Lyndon Lyon. Most rewarding under lights are the coral and dark blue hybrids, a type also well advanced by Mr. Lyon's work. Numerous miniatures thrive in 2–3-inch pots or in terrariums. All African-violets are easy to propagate by rooting leaves or dividing older plants that form several crowns. If you wish to grow plants for show or to hybridize them, you will find directions in *Helen Van Pelt Wilson's African-Violet Book* (Hawthorn Books, Inc.).

Seemannia latifolia. (4″–6″) This trailer grows from underground rhizomes and is active most of the year with glowing red tubular flowers, sparkling yellow at the throat. Plants are compact and at home in 3–4-inch pots with occasional pinching of stem tips.

Sinningia. (4″-6″; 10″ for miniatures) Most cultivated species in this tuberous genus come from tropical jungles

Miniature *Sinningia* 'Dollbaby'.

Miniature *Sinningia* 'Cindy Ella'.

where the tubers are under rich humus. Gloxinias, the large-flowered tuberous hybrids popular as gifts, are derived from sinningia species. Best under lights are the modern dwarf gloxinia hybrids and any of the true miniature sinningia species or their hybrids. The tiny sinningias are joining African-violets in popularity, so many new hybrids have been introduced. Charming in terrariums or 2–3-inch pots under lights are *S.pusilla* (light lavender, 1″–2″ tall), and *S.concinna* (speckled purple flowers). Hybrids of these include *S.* 'Bright Eyes' (constant succession of tiny lavender flowers), *S.* 'Cindy-Ella' (speckled trumpet-shaped lavender and white), and *S.* 'Dollbaby' (lavender, nearly everblooming). All grow from small underground tubers.

A recent change in nomenclature requires that several species long called *Rechsteineria* now be placed in the genus *Sinningia*. Two excellent light-garden species—technically no longer Rechsteinerias, although

Sinningia 'Robin Hood', bright-red flowers.

you will find them under that genus in many books—are *S.cardinalis* (light green velvety leaves, tubular red flowers), and *S.leucotricha*, called "Brazilian edelweiss" for the plush silvery leaves. *S.leucotricha* also has red flowers, but it is mainly grown for the unique foliage.

xGloxinera, formally listed as hybrids between *Rechsteineria* and *Sinningia*, are now called just *Sinningia*, but they are sold in some catalogues as *xGloxinera*. Good under lights are the hybrid 'Melinda' (2″ light lavender flowers with spotted throats) and 'Laurie', a white-flowered clone with a yellow throat. A rewarding larger species is *S.regina* which has deep purple slipper-shaped flowers, silver-veined foliage, charming under rosy-toned fluorescent lamps.

Miniature sinningias require less light to bloom and grow symmetrically than the large-flowered gloxinias and taller sinningias such as *S.cardinalis*. In contrast the larger gloxinias and hybrids with *S.eumorpha*, such as S. 'Melinda', S. 'Laurie', and similar sorts, will only develop compact floriferous plants if kept close to the lamps. Usually a site 4–6 inches below the center section of two or more 40-watt lamps will furnish enough intensity for show-quality gloxinias. With less light they get leggy, have fewer flowers.

After flowers fade from sinningias you can often obtain an immediate regrowth with a second crop of flowers by cutting back the first stem flush with the tuber top just as it starts to die. This works well with *S.cardinalis* and various miniature hybrids such as S. 'Bright Eyes'. When dormancy finally starts you can set the potted tubers in a dark place, 55°–65°. After 6–10 weeks bring them into growth with increased light, heat, and water.

Smithiantha. (3″–6″) These velvet-leaved gesneriads grow from rhizomes and will be dormant for one to two months in winter. Starting new rhizomes into growth from time to time (each scale will produce a plantlet) provides a constant supply of these "Temple bells" under lights. Usual potting is to put a whole rhizome in a 4- or 5-inch pot. The 1" yellow and orange spotted flowers are formed on upright spikes above foliage which, in many cultivars, is covered with maroon plush. Most suitable in the light garden are compact hybrids such as 'Little Tudor' and 'Little Wonder', two dwarfs with maroon foliage.

Streptocarpus. (3"–6") The most popular of these fibrous-rooted gesneriads are the compact 4–8-inch mutants of blue-flowered *Streptocarpus* 'Constant Nymph', a nearly everblooming Cape-primrose that forms clumps of 8–10-inch strap foliage. Florists offer *S.rexii* hybrids in white, purple, or pink, excellent under lights but growing to 10 inches tall.

Provide 55°–60° nights. Warmer temperatures are tolerated with adequate light during the day. Best under fluorescents are variations of 'Constant Nymph' such as 'Maasens White' (with yellow throat), 'Mini Nymph' (medium blue, compact growth), or 'Ultra Nymph' (largest flower, dark blue on compact plant). Add a teaspoon of dolomite limestone to each 4–5-inch pot of streptocarpus. Repot every year to give enough room for the vigorous roots characteristic of the 'Constant Nymph' mutations. Propagation is by division or by rooting leaves. You can also obtain seed from plant-society seed fund or from commercial growers and get flowering plants in six to nine months.

11

Orchids, All Year Long

Orchids were the first tropicals I grew under lights more than twenty years ago and they grew so well that fluorescents have become a permanent feature of my indoor growing systems. Success with orchids under lights begins when you select species and hybrids suited to the conditions you can provide.

Moderate to Strong Light

If you plan to grow orchids in a bookshelf garden, where moderate light is provided by two broad-spectrum lamps, select Moth orchids (*Phalaenopsis*) or ladyslippers (tropical *Paphiopedilum*), genera that thrive under medium light. If you want to grow *Ascocenda*, cattleya-type hybrids, bulbous *Epidendrum* totally under fluorescents, the light must be strong, as furnished by three or more 40-watt broad-spectrum lamps.

Some members of the American Orchid Society have experimented for years with fluorescents, many growing orchids in bright growth chambers or plant rooms. Del Hollenberg, for example, built a cabinet, painted it white inside, and installed banks of fluorescents 3 inches apart to provide a flood of light for cattleya hybrids. In fact, the intensity was so strong that his Moth orchids had to be shaded or placed to the sides where light falls off.

In my own collection many genera thrive under four 40-watt broad-spectrum lamps. In the greenhouse, where orchids receive some direct sun in the morning but only diffuse light after noon, I provide supplemental fluorescent light with two 40-watt lamps hung about 10 inches above the foliage. Some of my cattleya hybrids make growths under the medium light of only two lamps, yet produce satisfactory flowers. However, for certain bloom on a wide range of hybrids, I find fixtures with four lamps are better.

Light-Hour Variations

Most species are day-neutral and bloom well with 13 to 14 light-hours per 24 hour period. A few must have precise combinations of light or temperature changes to bloom freely. In the tropics orchids experience little change between night- and day-length. Species along the equator live with 12-hour days all year. Those in mountainous regions can still receive 15- to 60-minute variations between day and night according to season and topography. Although the official sunset may come at 6 P.M., orchids on a tree branch in the valley may be quite dark by 5 P.M.

If you have a collection of mature orchids from several genera, vary the light-hours slightly according to the season. Provide 16 to 18 hours of light from spring into late summer. In September reduce day-length to 14 hours, then to 12 hours November through January. As the year progresses, gradually increase the light to 16 hours by March or early April. This program will assure bloom on species that require a light duration change for flower bud initiation.

Phalaenopsis amabilis, the white Moth orchid, when grown with long nights at 65° minimum night temperature will often bloom more than once a year. With short nights, blooming is reduced to once a year. A smiliar reaction to long nights occurs with the pink Moth orchid *P.schilleriana*, and in *Dendrobium phalaenopsis*, an Asian species with round flowers resembling those of the Moth orchids.

Night Temperatures

Night temperatures no higher than 65° are important for maximum flowering, since warmer nights inhibit bloom, regardless of night-length. This is especially true for species from high altitudes and during the fall when many orchids are initiating buds. Tests to determine the complex interrelationships between temperature and dark periods have yet to be conducted with most orchids.

However we do know that *Cattleya warscewiczii* and *C.gaskelliana*, both large-flowered species that bloom as new growth matures, require long nights at 55° for maximum bloom. *Cattleya labiata*, an autumn-flowering species in the background of many hybrids, also needs 13-hour nights to initiate flowers, but temperatures are not so crucial and 60° – 65° nights are satisfactory.

Commercial Controls

Commercial growers capitalize on these reactions to achieve maximum bloom for Christmas, Easter, and Mother's Day. To hold back bloom on winter-flowering hybrids so as to have flowers for Easter, a grower would turn on lights for 2 to 3 extra hours of "day" in fall and winter. Lights might burn from 5:30 AM to 7:30 AM (sunrise), thus tricking plants into holding back bloom. About four months before flowers are wanted, a grower will stop extending the days and let his orchids bloom. Such commercial controls are impractical for a home collection.

Modern cattleyas and other popular orchids are often complex hybrids with several species or even different genera in their makeup, and these hybrids are not so predictable in their light-period reactions. Fortunately most of the orchids you are likely to grow will thrive without special manipulation of light hours.

My friends at Beall Orchids in Vashon, Washington report that most of their yellow, green, and art-shade cattleya hybrids bloom in summer as long-day plants. In my collection I have some new hybrids involving *Cattleya*, *Laelia*, *Brassavola*, and *Sophronitis*, a mixed bag of genera, producing plants with yellow to red-bronze flowers. These appear without fail every summer. Growths are made under the long days and short nights of spring and summer.

Another example is the butterfly-shaped *Oncidium* Kalihi (*O.papilio* X *O.kramerianum*), a favorite for its habit of flowering on and off throughout the year. A clump of this yellow-and-brown hybrid has grown for three years on a bright living-room window sill. It receives supplemental light from an overhead fluorescent that provides little intensity because I use it mainly to illuminate flowers at night.

However a side effect is that this orchid has had short nights all year round. Little intensity is required for plants to react as though it were still daytime. Unlike some of the pure cattleyas, which need slightly longer nights than days to bloom, this *Oncidium* hybrid has been a joy, producing one golden-and-brown ruffle-edged butterfly after another on long thin spikes. This is the kind of orchid that I feature in recommendations given later.

Faster Bloom

Seedling orchids grow faster under extended days. The world-famous nursery of Arthur Freed Orchids in Malibu, California employs artificial light over seedlings, to extend days to 18 light-hours. The head grower, Amado Vazquez, estimates that seedlings make four months' growth in three months' time thanks to the supplemental light. I use a similar program to extend days and raise light levels without risk of burning seedlings, as might occur with sunshine.

Since orchids may take five to six years to bloom from seed, any means of accelerating growth is valuable. Provide up to 18-hour days until plants reach maturity, then follow the schedule given before for mature plants. Fall and winter long nights, with 60°–65° temperatures, should prompt mature seedlings to bloom.

Your personal experiences with orchids under lights are of interest to the American Orchid Society. The A.O.S. sponsors research projects including studies to furnish new information about growing orchids under lights. The experience of home growers is sought for compilation and possible use in the monthly *American Orchid Society Bulletin.* If you have information that you think is of value, for example about certain species you find rewarding under specific light-garden conditions, send your notes to the American Orchid Society at the address listed in Chapter 21. The latest practical research with orchids under lights is reported in the monthly A.O.S. *Bulletin.* A collection of past studies will be found in *The Orchids, A Scientific Survey,* edited by Dr. Carl Withner (The Ronald Press Co., 1959).

Culture Basics

Epiphytes

Orchids such as Cattleyas and Phalaenopsis normally live on tree branches or mossy rocks in the tropics. These are epiphytic genera and require an airy compost. Mixtures of tree bark (fir or redwood), coarse perlite, and tree-fern fibers are easiest to use although some growers still pot in osmunda, a tough fern root. Commercial orchid growers sell ready-mixed orchid potting composts and the various ingredients too. Pot epiphytes in relatively small pots with at least 1 inch of gravel or crocks for drainage. Burn extra holes in plastic pots.

Terrestrials

Some orchids grow best with an airy humus-rich compost containing some soil. Species that live with rotted leaves around their roots, as in a tree crotch or on the forest floor, should be potted in a well-drained terrestrial orchid compost that stays slightly moist. These terrestrial growers, including *Cymbidium* and *Paphiopedilum*, can actually be potted in modified humus-rich soil, but should not be grown in straight soil as used for a geranium. Mixtures of chopped sphagnum moss, pasteurized loam, and tree barks are satisfactory and such composts are offered ready-made by many dealers.

Phalaenopsis and *Paphiopedilum* orchids thrive in this basement greenhouse with 14-hour days.

Humidity

A minimum humidity of 50 to 60 percent is necessary for healthy orchids. This moisture in the air can be furnished by growing plants in groups over moist gravel or perlite and by using a humidifier. (See Chapter 7 for details.)

Watering

Epiphytic orchids—cattleyas, epidendrums and oncidiums—often have swollen stems called pseudobulbs, that store moisture. In the wild during dry seasons they go weeks without water, kept alive by the stored moisture and light evening dews or mists. Such species can go a week or more without water if humidity holds to 50 percent. Other epiphytes, such as the Moth orchids, have no pseudobulbs so they must be kept evenly moist with only slight drying of the compost between soakings.

In no event must epiphytic orchids be kept wet. It is always better to let the roots dry slightly between waterings. Potting mixes of bark, perlite, and tree-fern drain quickly when used above adequate crocks or gravel. Plastic pots made for orchids have extra drainage holes in them as do clay orchid pots. Terrestrial orchids do well when kept evenly moist. Soak the compost but then let it dry slightly before watering again.

Fertilizing

Provide a slow-release balanced fertilizer (14–14–14) for orchids under lights as insurance against underfertilizing. Plants in bark will need some extra nitrogen, as in a 30–10–10 water-soluble formula. Substitute a low-nitrogen formula when plants have completed new growth to encourage bloom rather than continued vegetative growth. Apply no extra fertilizer to orchids that are resting, that is not making new growth.

Propagating

Species with pseudobulbs need at least two to four per clump. You can divide these types just as new roots appear. Cut through the rhizome with a sterile knife or precision shears. Dust the cut with Rootone and then pot. Orchids without pseudobulbs may produce plantlets on old inflorescences or alongside the main crown. Plantlets can be removed once they have roots several inches long, or let them remain with the large plant for a clump effect.

New hybrids and select species are propagated by seed sown on nutrient agar or by a modern vegetative process. A portion of the growing bud is cut out, then the tissue is cultured on nutrient agar. This process, called meristem propagation, provides thousands of plantlets genetically identical to the parent plant. Commercial dealers offer meristem plantlets of

Cattleya trianaei in a tropical Colombian habitat with faded flowers lower left, seedpot at top center. Roots run for a long distance along tree bark.

New roots just starting on *Cattleya* hybrid.

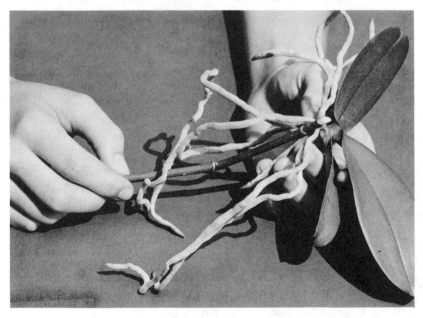

Phalaenopsis plantlet developed on the inflorescence has enough roots to be potted alone.

fine, often awarded, orchids at prices close to seedlings ($5 to $15). Before meristem propagation the same orchids sold for hundreds of dollars.

Orchids to Grow

The following genera and species are well suited to culture in light gardens. Unless otherwise noted, they are adaptable to intermediate 60°–65° nights. Especially good results can be obtained by supplementing sunlight with broad-spectrum fluorescents, but even with no daylight these orchids will prove rewarding under lights.

Aerangis. (6″–8″) Mainly dwarf monpodial (single crown) epiphytes from Africa and nearby islands in the Indian Ocean. *A.biloba* grows 3–5 inches, has 1-inch waxy-white, fragrant flowers. I grow a similar species, *A. compta*, on a small coffee tree just as it was found in Uganda. *A.rhodosticta* may reach 6 inches, has sprays of long-spurred white flowers with red centers. 65°–68° nights.

Angraecum. (4″–6″) Night-fragrant, white-flowered epiphytes from the same habitat as *Aerangis.* The angraecums bloom mainly in winter on 1 to 2 foot plants, somewhat tall for a light garden. *A.magdalenae* and *A. philippinense* (*Amesiella philippinensis*) are both dwarf, 6–8 inches, so hybrids with these smaller species and the popular large-flowered angraecums should produce some compact gems.

Ascocentrum. (2″–6″) Dwarf orange, yellow, red, or rose flowered epiphytes from tropical Asia, do best when they receive some sunlight or strong broad-spectrum fluorescents. Hybrids with *Vanda*, called *Ascocenda*, have an adaptable nature, compact 8- to 15-inch stems; they bloom several times a year with 65°–68° nights.

Mexican animalito pots are amusing, require careful watering since they have no drainage hole.

Aspasia. (4"–6") Epiphytes with 6–8-inch compact growth, fragrant waxy yellow, brown, and white flowers, long lasting. Try *A.principissa,* a spring-bloomer from Panama, or its excellent hybrid with *Brassia gireoudiana* (a Spider orchid), *Brapasia* Serene (fragrant 4-inch yellow flowers).

Brassavola. (2"–6") Central and South American epiphytes, tolerant of low humidity, adaptable. Species *B.nodosa,* called lady-of-the-night for its nocturnally fragrant white flowers, typically grows in strong sunlight but adapts to light culture with several flushes of bloom per year. Crosses of *B.nodosa* with *Cattleya* or *Laelia* inherit the compact close-growing habit, make fine hybrids for the light garden.

Brassia. (6"–8") The Spider orchids are epiphytes with yellow flowers, spotted brown, each having long spidery tepals—petals and sepals. *B.maculata* from Jamaica and Central America has sprays of fragrant, yellow-cream, 5- to 8-inch flowers dotted maroon. A good hybrid is *B.*Edvah Loo (*B.longissima* X *B.gireoudiana*) with 8- to 10-inch long flowers in spring and fall.

Catasetum. (4"–6") Deciduous Latin American epiphytes with fragrant, waxy flowers, usually either male or female but occasionally perfect (bisexual). Pot in small well-drained containers with tree-fern or bark mix, grow with 65°–68° nights. When the pseudobulbs stop producing leaves, gradually withhold water. Leaves will begin to fall as plants enter their four- to eight-week resting period. *C.pileatum,* the national flower of Venezuela, has 3- to 4-inch yellow-to-white, wide-lipped flowers in fall. *C.warscewiczii* is a 3–4-inch dwarf with a pendulous inflorescence of many 1½-inch greenish-white flowers. Recent hybrids are exciting and adaptable. Look for *Catasetum* Francis Nelson, a Beall company hybrid of

Catasetum Francis Nelson, new hybrid of *C.trulla* x *C.fimbriatum* created by the Beall Co. This was brown under a combination of daylight and fluorescents.

C.trulla X *C.fimbriatum*, and the Jones and Scully hybrid of *C.pileatum* X *C.expansum*, *C.* Orchidglade.

Cattleya. (3″–6″) These traditional corsage orchids often reach 2–3 feet, but with careful selection you can obtain compact species and their hybrids that bloom at 8–12 inches. All cattleyas are epiphytes with swollen pseudobulbs and thick white roots. Bright light is required for maximum bloom. Compact types include:

C.aclandiae, a Brazilian species with fragrant 3–4-inch flowers, 4–5-inch dwarf growth.

C.aurantiaca from Mexico and Central America has bright orange flowers in clusters, a characteristic passed on to its hybrids such as the rewarding Lc.Chit Chat 'Tangerine', available as a mericlone from the Fred Stewart company.

C.forbesii is a slender 10–12-inch plant from Brazil. Flowers are yellow with dark brown markings. I find primary hybrids of *C.forbesii* do well under lights.

C.intermedia, a spring-and summer-blooming species from Brazil, has waxy lavender flowers in clusters to splashed petals (var. *aquinii*), is available.

C.walkeriana has 3–5-inch stems but large 3–4-inch fragrant rose or white flowers. Hybrids are compact, too (see catelogue of Jones and Scully). Blooms mainly in winter.

The majority of cattleya species and their hybrids will produce maximum bloom under four to eight broad-spectrum lamps (i.e., Wide-Spectrum Gro-Lux) or with a combination of sunlight and fluorescents. IIybrids with *Sophronitis* are generally free-flowering and somewhat

Cattleya intermedia grows well under fluorescents.

more compact than straight cattleya or laeliocattleya hybrids. See the red hybrid on the front cover of this book. Excellent mericlones with compact habit include *Slc.*Brandywine 'Brilliant (deep purple-red), and *Slc.*Jewel Box 'Crimson Glory' (red flowers, winter to spring).

Comparettia macroplectron. (3″–6″) Although this epiphytic Colombian species is but 5–8 inches high, the arching flower spike may reach 24 inches, with an abundance of flat, light lavender 2-inch flowers, delicately spotted deep purple, usually in fall to early winter.

Cycnoches. (4″–6″) The Swan orchids resemble *Catasetum* and require the same culture. *C.ventricosum* var. *warscewiczii* and var. *chlorochilon* are both lovely with fragrant 5- to 7-inch yellow flowers. Any of the *Cycnoches* hybrids are fine under fluorescents.

Cymbidium. (3″–8″) Terrestrial growers with spikes of waxy, long-lasting blooms. For the most flowers select miniature oriental types or polymins, the hybrids between large cool-growing cymbidiums and small warm-growing species. Set plants outside from June to October. They will accept full sun except during midday when they should receive high shade as from tall trees. Indoors, give cymbidiums four to six broad-spectrum lamps which will have to be raised as spikes grow since even the miniatures have 15- to 20-inch inflorescences. Choose some of the proven clones now available as mericlones from firms listed in Chapter 21. Standard cymbidiums not only are too large for growing in most light gardens, but they also require cool 50° fall nights to set buds. The miniature and polymins do well with 60°–65° nights.

Dendrobium. (4″–6″) The dendrobiums differ so much in the requirements among species that you must consult orchid

Cycnodes Ginger Snap, with waxy brown-pink flowers, is a hybrid of *Cycnoches chlorochilon* and *Mormodes colossus*.

catalogues to select those suitable for your conditions. Among the most popular are the dwarf epiphytic *D.aggregatum* with bright yellow flowers in spring from dwarf growth, and the spectacular *D.nobile* hybrids that grow to two feet. The *D.nobile* hybrids require 50° nights in the fall to bloom well. The Yamamoto hybrids are an excellent strain. All dendrobiums do best in small clay pots with reduced watering when not in active growth. Some of the smaller species grow well on cork-bark slabs.

Epidendrum. (4″–8″) There are nearly 1,000 recognized *Epidendrum* species with several different growth habits. Best under lights are the compact epiphytes such as *E.anceps* with clusters of hay-scented green flowers, *E.ciliare* with white 3- to 6-inch fringed flowers several

Epidendrum cochleatum.

times per year, and the nearly everblooming *E.cochleatum*, the cockleshell orchid, with yellow-and-dark-maroon flowers. The semi-terrestrial reed-stem epidendrums are easy to grow but must nearly touch the tubes to bloom well. Crossing epidendrum species with cattleyas has created compact *Epicattleya* hybrids suitable for light gardens.

Laelia. (2″–4″) Laelias are epiphytes with flowers resembling small cattleyas. Numerous hybrids between *Laelia* and *Cattleya* have created an abundance of unusual showy orchids. Pure species to grow under lights include *L.pumila*, a dwarf Brazilian with round, sparkling, lavender flowers, and the white to lavender *L.rubescens* from Central America, best on a slab of cork bark.

Sophrolaelia Psyche is a 6-inch tall red-orange hybrid which blooms several times a year under lights.

Lepanthes. (6″–8″) These epiphytes are true miniatures, ½–1 inch tall with tiny jewel-like yellow, green, or maroon flowers on short spikes. Provide cool-to-intermediate (55°–65°) nights and high humidity. Species are fine in an open-top terrarium under lights or in large glass Wardian cases. In pots use very small clay kinds with unmilled sphagnum moss or tree-fern fiber, maintained evenly moist. Similar miniatures to grow with *Lepanthes* are *Masdevallia* and *Pleurothallis*.

Miltonia. (6″–8″) Miltonias are epiphytes with sprays of flat flowers, sometimes called Pansy orchids for the face-like markings. Species from lowland Brazil (*M.clowesii, M.spectabilis*) have 2–4-inch flowers that pick well. The large-flowered, cool-growing species and their hybrids (*M.vexillaria, M.roezlii*) from higher altitudes last well only on the plant. All the miltonias, especially the vigorous hybrids, are suitable for light gardens. Look for *Miltonia* Goodale Moir, a nice yellow, warm-growing hybrid and M.Bremen, a striking red-and-white, cool-growing hybrid. *Miltassia* is an excellent hybrid genus with *Brassia*, blooming on and off all year.

Neofinetia falcata. (4″–8″) This 6–8-inch epiphyte looks like a tiny *Vanda* with ridged succulent foliage forming small monopodial fans. Pristine white flowers with long "tails" appear on 4–6-inch spikes, have a vanilla perfume. Hybrids with a similar dwarf growth include *Ascofinetia* (x*Ascocentrum*) and *Nakamotoara* (x*Ascocentrum* and *Vanda*). Keep roots evenly moist since these have no pseudobulbs.

Odontoglossum. (6″–8″) Some *Odontoglossum* species from Mexico and Central America thrive with intermediate temperatures, but the classic *Odm.crispum* hybrids, created from Andean species, must have cool 55°–60° nights. However these epiphytes are all good choices for light gardens since they bloom well and grow easily in small pots of tree-fern or unmilled sphagnum moss. Newer crosses combine other genera into manmade hybrids, usually more adaptable than straight species or plain cool-growing strains. Look for *Aspoglossum* (x *Aspasia*), *Colmanara* (x*Miltonia* and *Oncidium*), and *Odontocidium* (x *Oncidium*). The Beall Co. lists a large selection of such hybrids.

Oncidium. (3″–6″) Most oncidiums have sprays of 1–3-inch flowers with bright yellow lips. Grow these epiphytes in small pots of bark or tree-fern and give good air circulation. Nice under lights are compact species such as *O.ampliatum* (very strong light), *O.cheirophorum*, a dwarf with fragrant yellow flowers fall into winter, and *O.ornithorhynchum* with sprays of fragrant rose flowers. *O.Goldiana* (*O.flexuosum* X *O.sphacelatum*) is a robust yet compact hybrid with sprays of golden flowers.

Ornithocephalus. (4″–6″) Miniature epiphytes, best grown on slabs of tree-fern. The common name Mealybug orchid refers to tightly-packed spikes of fuzzy white flowers. Plants produce a flat fan of succulent foliage, interesting in itself. *O.bicornis* is 1–3 inches, *O.grandiflorus* grows 4–6 inches. Look at the flowers under a magnifying glass.

Paphiopedilum. (4″–8″) The tropical ladyslipper orchids grow as terrestrials on the jungle floor, on steep banks above streams, or in mossy glens. They thrive under fluorescent lights and flowers last three to eight weeks on the plant. Some kinds have tesselated (marked with squares) foliage of deep green or silver, attractive all year. Paphiopedilums are favored for black warts, erect stems, waxy pouches, and glossy hairs. If such features

146

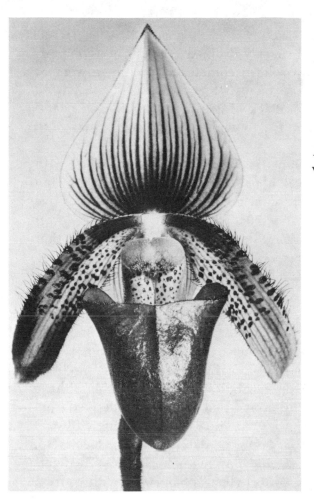

Paphiopedilum ciliolare from warm Philippine jungles.

hardly evoke images of beauty you must see how nature combines these parts. Some ladyslippers have vertical stripes of white and green on the wide top sepal. Many species and their hybrids have black hairs all along the two side petals. The smooth plump pouch is a distinguishing feature of all paphiopedilums.

Intermediate to warm nights are suitable for those species and hybrids with mottled foliage (*P.concolor, P.Maudiae, et al.*), while kinds with plain green leaves make sturdier growth at 55°-60°.

Pot in a sharply-drained terrestrial compost. Suitable mixes are sold by commercial orchid growers, or you can make your own with equal parts of medium to fine orchid bark, Black Magic planter mix, and coarse perlite. Keep roots evenly moist, but do not let pots set in water.

Paphiopedilums need bright diffuse light, with relative humidity of at least 50 percent. The cool-growing ladyslippers, with plain green leaves, are more sensitive to low temperatures (50°–55° nights) for setting flower buds than to day-length. Studies with *P.insigne* show that this cool-growing species blooms well with short or long days if nights drop to at least 55°. The same species exposed to 65° night temperature did not set flower buds on long *or* short days. Such a temperature response (thermo-induction) of flower buds also occurs in standard cymbidium orchids that need cool nights to bloom.

Select the warmer-growing species and their hybrids unless you can drop the night temperatures to 55°. I have a collection of unusual mottled-leaf hybrids derived from tropical Asian species that thrive under lights with 65° nights. Hybrids are more adaptable than species so, although pure *P.insigne* may require cool 50°–55° nights to set buds, some of its hybrids bloom well with warmer intermediate nights.

P.bellatulum is a dwarf-growing, warm-preference species from Thailand with creamy flowers, lightly speckled maroon. Leaves are tesselated with dark green. Similar species for intermediate to warm nights are *P.concolor* and *P.niveum*. All three are summer-blooming but under lights may have flowers at other seasons too.

P.glaucophyllum from Java has glaucous leaves, produces dark green and maroon flowers with hairy twisted petals on and off during the whole year.

P.sukhakulii is a variable colored species from Thailand but it always has lovely mottled foliage and flowers with a pointed yellow-and-rose-blushed pouch, white-to-yellow toned petals with pubescent margins, dark maroon dots.

P.venustum is a dwarf Himalayan species valuable for the thick mottled foliage, deep purple underneath, and 2- to 3-inch waxy purple, green, and yellow flowers with a veined pouch.

Phalaenopsis. (6″–10″) Moth orchids are excellent for light gardens because the flowers last for weeks and plants are flat and low growing. They thrive with less light than many showy orchids. Phalaenopsis are epiphytes, grow well in bark or tree-fern mixes, but must be kept lightly moist since they have no pseudobulbs. You will be pleased with any of them, especially the striking modern hybrids in white, yellow, pink, or combinations with stripes or deep-colored lips. Among compact species are *P.lueddemanniana* with fragrant, waxy, red-barred flowers and *P.violacea* with 2- to 3-inch white flowers marked purple and green. Hybrids of these species tend to be more compact than standard white or pink selections.

When flowers fade, cut back the 1- to 3-foot inflorescence to just above a lower node. This often prompts the plant to sprout a secondary inflorescence and thus double your flower production. Hybrids with related genera are adaptable, exciting in the light garden. Look for *Asconopsis* (x*Ascocentrum*), *Doritaenopsis* (xDoritis), and *Renanthopsis* (xRenanthera). (See color plate of *Phalaenopsis* with African violets on front cover.)

Pleurothallis. (4″–8″) These are generally dwarf 2–6-inch plants forming tufts of foliage with small sprays of tiny

Pleurothallis lanceola, grown to perfection by Phil Jesup, a specialist in miniature orchids, is typical of this compact genus.

flowers, best appreciated under a magnifying glass. Charming cool to intermediate epiphytes for limited space, often thrive mounted on slabs of tree fern or in 1- or 2-inch thumb pots.

Polystachya. (4″-8″) This is one of the few genera to be found in both the Old and New World tropics. Species are epiphytes that thrive in small pots of tree-fern or unmilled sphagnum. *P.luteola* has 8- to 10-inch erect spikes of fragrant, yellow-green flowers on compact 8- to 12-inch plants. *P.phalax* is fragrant, white with yellow-and-red markings, dwarf growth.

Rodriguezia. (4″-8″) These intermediate to warm-growing epiphytes thrive on slabs of tree-fern or in small pots of tree-fern, seldom grow above 6 inches, but arching flower spikes may reach 10 inches. *R.granadensis* from Colombia has 2-inch white flowers with yellow in the lip. (*R.venusta* is similar.) *R.secunda* bears 1-inch bright rose flowers several times during the year. Hybrids with *Oncidium*, called *Rodricidium*, are dwarf and free-flowering, excellent under lights.

Sarcochilus falcatus. (4″-6″) The Australian Orange blossom orchid has short spikes of fragrant white flowers dotted red, winter to spring. Plants are compact, do well on tree-fern, cork bark, or in small pots, grown under warm humid conditions.

Sophronitis. (6″-8″) Orange-and-red flowers have made these dwarf Brazilian epiphytes famous as parents. Sophronitis is bred with the much larger cattleyas, laelias, brassavolas, and related genera to impart dark orange to flame tones and dwarf growth to hybrids. Straight species are not easy, but with high humidity and culture on bark slabs or logs they can be grown under lights. Fall-to-winter blooming *S.cernua* (1-inch orange-red) and *S.coccinea* (syn. *S.grandiflora*) with vermilion 1- to 3-inch flowers are available from species specialists listed in Chapter 21.

Stanhopea. (6″-8″) Stanhopeas grow wide, dark green leaves to 12 inches long, from round pseudobulbs. Large 3- to 5-inch fragrant waxy flowers in white, yellow, or cream with maroon dots open on a spike that grows directly down from the bulbs. Pot in an open-slat basket with tree-fern, sphagnum moss strands, or osmunda fiber; suspend the basket under lamps. Although stanhopeas are too large for many light gardens, they are easy to grow and require only moderate light to bloom well. Spectacular, although lasting only five to eight days are *S.oculata* (vanilla- or chocolate-scented, 4- to 5-inch red-purple flowers in summer), and *S.eburnea* (fragrant 5- to 6-inch white flowers in fall).

Stelis. (6″–8″) This genus contains almost 500 species, mostly ½- to 4-inch epiphytes with sprays of small cream-to-yellow flowers. I have seen plants growing on moss-covered rocks and on twigs in cloud forests of South America. Thus in captivity they need high humidity, cool to intermediate nights, and sharp drainage. Pot in un-milled sphagnum moss, or mount on slabs of tree fern. They are at home in a collection of similarly dwarf *Pleurothallis* species. For full appreciation, study the flowers under magnification.

Foliage Orchids

Several terrestrial or ground-dwelling orchids are treasured for their jewel-like foliage. They do well under medium light, even with Cool White-Warm White combinations. A terrarium is also excellent for these low-growing Jewel orchids. All are tropical except the rattlesnake-plantain (*Goodyera pubescens*), a native of eastern North America. Pot these small terrestrials in humus-rich soil. Keep roots evenly moist but never soggy, humidity 60–70 percent. *Anoectochilus roxburghii* and *A.sikkimensis* are similar Far Eastern creepers with bronze-green foliage netted gold. One of my plants thrives with small ferns in a dish garden.

The rattlesnake-plaintain, has deep green foliage with fine silver lines. It is a cold-hardy native and long a favorite for New England partridge-berry terrariums. I find it does well with diffuse light and a temperature range of 50°–70°. It provides several years of beauty in a terrarium landscape under fluorescents.

Ludisia discolor, known for years as *Haemaria discolor*, is a robust Malayan species with dark purple-green leaves netted red or gold. Specimens may reach 8 inches, with the white flowers appearing on short spikes from the velvety new growth.

12

Geraniums for Bloom and Scent

The flowering geraniums we grow indoors, scientifically *Pelargonium*, perform well under broad-spectrum fluorescents and in situations where sun is supplemented with fluorescents. Some are miniature or dwarf, easy to keep 2 to 6 inches under lamps for top flower production. Less demanding are the foliage pelargoniums, grown for their scented leaves. The tall, older hybrids are less satisfactory under lights.

Potting

Although geraniums traditionally grow in heavy potting soils, I find they thrive for me in the basic mix or one of the commercial formulas such as Black Magic. Select small pots in relation to top growth so roots can fill the containers. Let the soil almost dry out between watering; keep humidity to 40–60 percent.

Temperature

Nights 55°–65° are suitable. Geraniums grow sturdy with cool nights, light-hour temperatures about 10° higher.

Fragrant foliage types accept somewhat more warmth and more moisture at the roots because they can be so easily pinched when you harvest the perfumed leaves. *P.domesticum* hybrids must have 50°–55° nights for abundant bloom, and these regal or Martha Washington hybrids will accept nights to 45°, excellent for unheated light gardens.

Light and Fertilizer

Keep foliage 4–6 inches below broad-spectrum lamps. Apply a fertilizer higher in phosphorus and potash than nitrogen, like Hyponex 7–6–19 at one-quarter to one-half strength every third watering. Slow-release products are also suitable.

Night-Length

Give standard geraniums (*P.hortorum* hybrids), the miniatures, and scented-leaf types 14–16 hours of light per 24-hour period. *P.domesticum* hybrids *grow* well with 14 hours of light but must have 12–13 hour nights to set flower buds. After four to six weeks of long nights they wait for 13–14 hours *days* before flowers open. The easier *P.hortorum* and many miniature hybrids do not require such changes to bloom well under lights.

Propagation

Put tip cuttings, after the cut end has dried for a day, into the rooting mix. Older bushy specimens can be divided. Some of the best new flowering hybrids are available as seed. The Carefree geraniums come in thirteen colors and, when grown with 14 hour days 60°–65° nights, usually bloom in eight to ten weeks.

Pelargonium 'Apple Blossom Rosebud', a refined pink color.

Chemical Dwarfing

Cycocel chemical treatment will restrict rapid growth of geraniums, begonias, and other ornamental houseplants. This liquid control is widely used by commercial growers for plants that might become too tall unless given low night temperatures, very strong light, and pinching. Mix Cycocel with water according to directions, usually a dilution of one part Cycocel liquid to forty parts water. About one ounce of this dilution poured around plants will usually suffice to control growth.

Without Cycocel you can keep seedlings compact by pinching top growth once when several leaves have formed.

Grow seedlings 4 inches below tubes with nights as low as 50°. Warmer nights encourage taller plants.

Year to Year

Geraniums are at their best when young. To maintain a favorite clone, make tip cuttings at least every two years. Miniatures are so slow growing that they will continue for three to four years in the same pot but they too can be propagated to get vigorous young plants from tip cuttings. *P.domesticum* hybrids may be slow from cuttings, but new shoots will appear if old stems are cut down after flowers have faded. Leave 4- to 6-inch stubs to sprout into new stems.

Cultivars to Grow

Standard hybrids good under lights include the Carefree strain and similar heat-resistant modern hybrids.

Dwarfs and Miniatures

'Alpha', a semi-trailing hybrid with single red flowers, yellow-green leaves marked with darker ring.
'Arcturus', glowing double scarlet, 3–6-inch plant.
'Artic Star', pure white starry flowers, 4–6-inch treelike dwarf.

Ornamental Foliage

'Mrs. Henry Cox', brilliant combination of gold, red, white, and green.

My photogram shows scented *Pelargonium* 'Little Gem' (medium-sized leaf), 'Dr. Livingston' (largest), and 'Scarboroviae,' the strawberry geranium (small). All are life size.

Fragrant Foliage

Pelargonium crispum 'Prince Rupert Variegated', crinkled green-and-white foliage, lemon fragrance.

P.graveolens 'Little Gem', bushy habit, much cut fuzzy foliage with pungent smell, pink flowers.

P.radens 'Dr. Livingston', vigorous, lemon-scented, 2–3-inch skeleton-cut leaf.

P. x scarboroviae 'Countess of Scarborough', 1-inch glossy crinkled leaves with light fruity fragrance, strawberry to some.

13

A Gourmet's Garden of Herbs

Herbs thrive under fluorescent lights with cool to intermediate temperatures. A kitchen window with an overhead lamp, a cool room with a fluorescent growth fixture, a basement light garden—these are all suitable locations for an assortment of herbs. The best species to select are the compact growers and those varieties that are most frequently called for in recipes. Give broad-spectrum fluorescent light 14 to 16 hours per day or combine fluorescents with sunlight. Set plants 3 to 6 inches below lights.

Kinds to Enjoy

Basil (*Ocimum basilicum*). Usually grown as an annual from seed, these plants may live for several years if tops are pinched back to the first set of leaves; this prevents flowering, encourages new shoots. Purple 'Dark Opal' (*O. minimum* var.) is a form of bush basil, a nice contrast with the standard green form.

Bay leaf (*Laurus nobilis*). A Mediterranean shrub that endures cold into the 40's, has shiny, 2- to 4-inch, aromatic evergreen

Herbs thrive in a kitchen where humidity is usually high. These grow under two 20-watt lamps below a cabinet.

leaves. Provide even moisture, good air circulation, cool nights. Start as small plants from a nursery. Prune to any shape you wish, use leaves in soup, or make a crown for your hero.

Chives (*Allium schoenoprasum*). Chives are easy to grow outside or in and are one of the most useful herbs. Flowers that form in May and June are starry lilac balls soon followed by seed that will germinate quickly for an abundance of chivelets. Snip stems up to three quarters back; they will resprout from underground bulbs.

Marjoram (*M.hortensis*). This is the tender sweet form with gray foliage, stems 15–18 inches. Let soil almost dry out between waterings.

Mint (*Mentha* cultivars). *M.citrata*, the orange mint, has smooth, fragrant, purple-tinted foliage, delightful in cool drinks. Fuzzy leaves of *M.rotundifolia* have a fruity pineapple-mint flavor. Both are cold-hardy.

Oregano (*Origanum vulgare*). A tender perennial available as small plants from nurseries or grown from seed. Pinch tops for bushy growth. Use foliage in tomato sauce, Italian dishes. Replace after two to three years when stem gets woody.

Parsley (*Petroselinum hortense*). Universal garnish, available in plain leaf (*P.carnum*), and the more popular curled variety,

Some of the herbs to grow under lights include (from top left on rice paddle): sweet marjoram, chevril, lemon thyme, orange mint, parsley, rosemary, sweet basil, purple sage. In center are chives with chive flower cluster.

'Paramount'. Parsley is biennial, will die the second year once it has an opportunity to bloom. Cut out flowering tops to prolong life of the clump. Pick outside stems for garnish; new growths appear from center. Easy to grow when seed is soaked a day before planting.

Rosemary (*Rosmarinus officianalis*). A long-lived, blue-flowered shrub from southern Europe through Asia Minor, famous for thick aromatic gray leaves long before Ophelia cried "There's rosemary, that's for remembrance; pray you, love, remember." In a less tragic mood, it's fun to send sprigs of rosemary in letters, and the fragrant leaves are a delight in many dishes. Cool 50°–55° nights are best. Pinch fresh growth but don't prune severely into hardwood.

Sage (*Salvia officianalis, S.rutilans*). The hardy perennial *S.officianalis* has plain green leaves, shrubby growth to 12 inches, blue flowers. *S.rutilans*, the pineapple-flavored sage, is a semitropical from Mexico with scarlet flowers. Mix a tablespoon of dolomite limestone in each 6-inch pot of sage soil. Keep plants evenly moist, cut back as desired.

Thyme (*Thymus vulgaris* cultivars). These fragrant creepers grow best with broad-spectrum lamps, winter nights under 65°, sharply drained soil *T.* 'Golden Lemon' with variegated lemon-scented foliage, *T.serpyllum*, a low rosy-flowered form, and 'Caprilands' with the fragrance of several species are all pleasant.

14
A Foliage Rainbow

Foliage plants are stars under artificial light where the green leaves prosper with the lowest intensities accepted by any houseplants. Even bright-colored or variegated species don't need as much light as flowering plants. Thousands of graceful *Philodendron oxycardium* vines happily produce their heart-shaped leaves year after year creating islands of green on office desks around the world, all with nothing more than fluorescent ceiling lamps.

Similar survival stories can be told of pothos vines, palms, ferns, and aspidistras. In your light garden the foliage plants are excellent for filling in along the edges or the ends of fixtures. Bookshelf gardens with one lamp will look lovely with creeping fig, peperomias, and ferns. One of the most popular ways to use artificial light with foliage plants is as a supplement to daylight.

Reflector Incandescents

Tall rubber or weeping fig trees are not suitable in a light-garden cart but they frequently thrive where overhead reflector bulbs give light for 12 to 14 hours a day. Even big shrubs in

Syngonium podophyllum thrives in a Tufflite foam pot with lacy *Selaginella uncinata*, both low-light requirement species.

heavy tubs can be set on casters and turned every few days for even growth. Reflector bulbs in the ceiling also provide dramatic lighting at night and help plants grow better in dim weather.

Although light from fluorescent lamps drops off quite rapidly as distance increases, they may still be used to supplement daylight, especially for low-light level species such as ivies, philodendrons, ferns, many palms, spathiphyllums, and syngoniums.

Vertically placed fluorescent tubes in walls are useful for tall foliage plants. Conceal the lamps with panels of frosted Plexiglas (available in several colors but clear is best for plants). Some delightful foliage effects can be created with the following plants; those marked* will also grow in one-quarter-strength water-soluble fertilizer solution for many months.

Coleus salicifolius, a red cultivar grown from seed under lights, responds well to various types of fluorescent tubes.

Alocasia 'Amazonica'
(*A. sanderiana* X
A. lowii grandis).

Alocasia. (8″–10″) Tuberous warm-growing plants with caladium-shaped foliage, bold veins on dark green or metallic background, often with glossy sheen.

Anthurium. (6″–10″) Warm-growing, semi-epiphytic jungle plants with strap leaves in *A.bakeri*, rounded, heavy, deep green with silver veins in *A.clarinevium* and *A.crystallinum*.

Biophytum sensitivum. (6″–8″) An oxalis relative resembling a 3-6-inch palm tree, suitable for landscapes in terrariums or small light gardens. Ripe pods shoot seed several feet.

Buxus microphylla japonica. (6″–10″) This miniature boxwood makes a bushy shrub *when pruned* but eventually can reach 5–6 feet. Endures cold nights.

Caladium. (4″–10″) Multicolored lance-shaped foliage on 10–15-inch stems from underground tubers. Dormant two to three months each year but can rest in pots. *C.humboldtii* is a green-and-white miniature.

Caladium 'Candidum'.

Calathea picturata
Argentea'.

Calathea. (8″–10″) Jungle floor *Maranta* relative for warm humid locations. Clumps of multicolored foliage. *C.picturata* 'Argentea' is compact with silver leaves edged dark green, red-blushed underneath.

Carissa grandiflora var. *nana compacta.* (4″–8″) Natal plum. Glossy thick foliage, spiny twigs, starry white flowers, red edible fruit.

Chamaedorea elegans 'Bella'. (8″–12″) A dwarf palm, adaptable, and slow-growing.

Chlorophytum comosum. (6″–10″) Spider plants form runners with small plantlets and white flowers. Largest is *C.variegatum* with white-edged leaves; *C.vittatum* is a compact 4–6-inch plant with leaves banded white in the center.

Chlorophytum comosum vittatum.

Codiaeum variegatum. (4″–8″) The crotons are tropical shrubs with strap- or oak-shaped, shiny leaves in various colors, depending upon variety. 'Punctatum aureum', is a retrained miniature with narrow leaves flecked gold.

Coffea arabica. (6″–12″) Coffee shrubs have glossy foliage, white fragrant flowers, red "cherries." Prune to keep compact.

*Coleus blumei hybrids. (4″–8″) Bright-colored foliage in various shapes, depending upon type. Grow an assortment from seed; every 12–15 months, propagate the colors you like best with stems rooted in water. Spires of blue flowers if not pinched back. Vibrant under rosy Gro-Lux.

*Dieffenbachia. (6″–12″) The dumbcanes grow 2–4 feet tall but can be shortened by rooting tops of leggy plants. Young plants are good in light gardens.

Dizygotheca elegantissima. (8"-10") Sometimes called spider-aralia for palmy fringed leaves. Leggy plants can be air-layered.

Dracaena. (6"–8") Best under lights are compact sorts such as *D.godseffiana* 'Florida Beauty', a slow-growing dark green with many cream spots and *D.goldieana*, with zebra-striped foliage. The thin upright *D.sanderiana* resembles a corn plant with white-margined leaves.

Ficus diversifolia. (8"-10") This thick-leaved ornamental fig has small yellow fruit, restrained shrubby habit, best fig for light gardens.

Fittonia verschaffeltii. (12"-15") Dwarf creeper for warm, humid light gardens, deep green leaves with red or white veins.

Hypoestes sanguinolenta. (4"-6") Polkadot plants thrive the same way as coleus, have pink-spotted, deep green leaves, lavender flowers.

Melaleuca hypericifolia. (4"-8") Really a tall tree but with pinching this forms a shrub. Gray-and-tan bark is attractive, foliage smells like menthol, accepts cool nights.

Mimosa pudica. (4"-6") This sensitive plant is a lively delight, responding to touch by folding its leaves. Grow from seed without transplanting. Usually dies in twelve to fifteen months after blooming.

Osmanthus fragrans. (4"-8") The fragrant olive is a smooth-leaved shrub with tiny white flowers perfumed like orange blossoms, best with cool nights. *O.ilicifolius variegatus* is hollylike, with cream-edged spiny foliage.

Oxalis hedysaroides rubra. (4"-8") Sometimes called firefern for its brilliant, deep maroon leaves. Adaptable to various

Maranta leuconeura kerchoveana thrives with thsame culture as for *Calathea*.

Oxalis martiana 'Aureo-Reticulata'.

temperatures but resents being shifted once it is established. Chrome-yellow flowers appear through the year. *O.martiana aureo-reticulata* grows from a scaley bulb into a clump of cloverlike, golden striped leaves. Flowers are pink. May go dormant for several weeks.

Peperomia. (6″–10″) Nearly all the dwarf or miniature peperomias are delightful under lights, easy to propagate from leaf cuttings. Very colorful is *P.sandersii* with round silver-banded leaves.

Plectranthus coleioides marginatus (top, larger leaf) and the variety *minima* thrive under lights with minimum care.

Philodendron. (8″–15″) Some species such as *P.wendlandii* make full crowns of glossy leaves; these are corrugated in the hybrid 'Lynette', but most species offered are the trailing or climbing types. New cultivars are available with maroon or black-red toned foliage.

Polyscias. (8″–10″) Fringed and frilly foliage on plants that resemble small trees after several years, but with pinching usually remain under two feet. *P.fruticosa elegans* and *P.guilfoylei victoriae* are rewarding under lights.

Ruellia makoyana. (6″–8″) This ruellia has dark magenta flowers, purple-olive foliage, purple underneath, silver veins. Provide warm humid conditions, propagate from tip cuttings.

Schefflera actinophylla (Brassaia). (6″–12″) Seedlings and small cuttings of this Australian tree fit light gardens, older specimens are best in floor planters lit by diffuse daylight and overhead artificial light from spots or fluorescents.

Saxifraga stolonifera (Syn. *sarmentosa*) the Strawberry-begonia is neither begonia nor strawberry but it *is* an attractive, clump-forming foliage plant. Variety 'Tricolor' is blushed deep pink on white leaf edges. Let it dry out slightly between waterings.

Strobilanthes dyerianus. (8"–10") The Persian-shield is named for its iridescent blue, silver, and purple foliage, best under warm humid conditions.

Trailers, Creepers, and Climbers

Graceful trailing greenery creates a jungle effect by softening straight lines on light stands, moisture trays, and similar mechanical aspects of the light garden. Charming combinations are possible with compatible species, mixing trailers around the base of tall plants, or planting a green trailer, such as *Begonia solanthera* with bronze *Pilea repens*. Some foliage plants which trail or twine can grow for months in a solution of weak fertilizer or even water alone. These are marked*.

Cissus. (6"–10") Grape-ivies grow with ease under cool-to-intermediate temperatures. *C.antarica* and *C.rhombifolia* are large leaved; *C.striata* is a true miniature for a limited space.

Cyanotis. (8"–12") The inch-plants are creepers but slower than zebrina. *C.kewensis* has golden-brown plush leaves, *C.somaliensis*, silvery leaves, very fuzzy.

Cymbalaria muralis. (6"–10") Kenilworth-ivy is a dainty but vigorous trailer best grown around the base of a tall plant or trained on a trellis. Small one quarter-inch, white to dark lavender flowers like tiny snapdragons. Sow seed where plants are to grow.

Ficus pumila. (6"–12") The miniature creeping fig is delightful trained over small rocks or on driftwood. An oakleaf form is available. All types have pebbly, deep green leaves; *F.pumila minia* and *F.pumila quercifolia* are the smallest.

Ficus pumila minima on driftwood.

Gynura aurantiaca. (6″–8″) The plush purple leaves earn this trailer the popular name of velvet-passion-vine. Easy under lights; propagate from tip cuttings in water.

Hedera helix cultivars. (8″–12″) English ivy comes in many interesting leaf forms and colors. Delightful under lights is the bushy dwarf 'Itsy Bitsy'. 'Conglomerata' looks good in a low bonsai container. Most cultivars are cold-hardy so will endure chilly nights.

Pellionia daveauana. (8″–10″) This has shiny metallic-bronze foliage marked green, nice around taller plants or in a terrarium. Slower is *P. pulchra* with blue-gray matte leaves marked with black lines, succulent pink stems.

Philodendron. (8″–15″) Easy vines for any situation with 50 percent humidity.

Pilea. (8″–12″) Creepers mainly useful in terrariums or small shelf gardens. *P.involucrata* and *P.repens* are bronze-toned, easy-growing species.

Setcreasea purpurea. (5″–8″) The purple-heart-vine thrives with bright or dim light but produces its orchid-colored flowers only with high intensity. Very lovely under Gro-Lux.

Syngonium. (10″–15″) The most adaptable low-light vine I can imagine, available in several cultivars with varying degrees of cream or white markings in the foliage. Most popular are cultivars of *S.podophyllum*.

Tradescantia (10″–15″) The wandering jews resemble zebrina species, are just as easy to grow around the base of taller plants or alone. *T.albiflora* has white-banded foliage; *T.blossfeldiana* tough, olive-green leaves, purple underneath, pale pink flowers. *T.sillamontana* has silvery plush leaves.

Zebrina. (10″–15″) The striped wandering jews are excellent around the base of small shrubs or massed in the moisture tray to conceal pots. Cultivars vary in arrangement of stripes; all are variations of purple, green, silver, and pink.

Ferns

The graceful green fronds of ferns blend well with other houseplants and serve to hide plain clay pots and to fill in between flowering specimens. Most ferns require low light; a few will accept bright light if they are gradually exposed. Some interesting types for the light garden are:

Tradescantia fluminensis variegata.

Tradescantia velutina photographed in its native Guatemala.

Pteris multifida variety, an adaptable fern for low to medium light, growing with a seedling of *Anthurium crystallinum*.

Adiantum. (6″–12″) The maidenhair ferns are delicate looking with filmy fronds of small thin leaflets on thin black stems. Compact are *A.hispidulum* and *A.tenerum* 'Wrightii'.

Asparagus densiflorus (syn. *A.meyeri*). (6″–10″) Looks like a full green foxtail. Tiny green flowers are followed by orange berries, a compact delight. Botanically a true asparagus.

Davallia. (6″–12″) The creeping rhizomes look like a rabbit's fuzzy feet; fronds are graceful with multicut leaves. Compact are *D.bullata mariesii* (grow with 65°–70° nights) and *D.pentaphylla*, the dwarf rabbit's-foot fern.

Nephrolepsis. (8″–15″) The many varieties of Boston ferns are cultivars of *N.exaltata*. 'Fluffy Ruffles' is a nice semidwarf. *N.cordifolia* 'Duffii' is a thin-fronded dwarf type with nearly round leaflets, nice in terrariums or in smaller light gardens.

178

Platycerium. (6″–10″) Any of the staghorn or elkhorn ferns are easy under lights with high humidity and sharp drainage.

Polystichum tsus-simense. (6″–12″) Dwarf holly fern with elegant restrained 6–8-inch fronds, slow-growing.

15

Begonias for Flowers and Foliage

The begonia family is so large that it can provide a nonstop parade of flowers and foliage color from miniature creeping species to towering angelwing cane types. Propagation is easy by seed, stem cuttings, and often from leaves as with the bright rex hybrids. Even more important in light gardens, many choice begonias are miniatures or very compact growers.

Roots are shallow and fibrous so grow begonias in bulb pans or three quarter-size pots. Intermediate 65°–68° nights and 50–60 percent humidity are ideal for most species. Semperflorens (wax begonias) and cane types accept slightly dryer, cooler conditions while the rexes are best with warm humid locations.

Lamps and Light-Hours

Foliage types do well with the Cool White-Warm White combination, but colors look much brighter under Gro-Lux or Agro-Lite tubes. Begonias grown mainly for flowers do well with broad-spectrum tubes.

Provide 14–16 hours of light per 24-hour period for growth. Seedlings and propagations move along faster with 16–18 hours of light. With relatively short 8–9-hour nights the summer-

Begonias in many sizes thrive throughout this unique light-garden room created by Jack Golding, president of the Indoor Light Gardening Society. Wedged louvers hide fluorescent lamps which cover the entire ceiling. Light-colored gravel and mirrored walls reflect maximum brilliance onto foliage from all sides. The ceiling looks dark in the distance due to the camera angle in relation to the louver wedge openings.

Begonia 'Improved Schwabenland Orange', a Rieger hybrid, produced the most flowers under Wide-Spectrum Gro-Lux lamps.

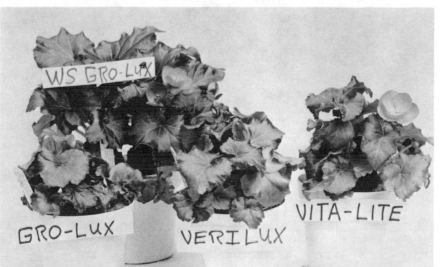

blooming tuberous begonias, rex hybrids, semperflorens (wax) hybrids, cane-stem or angelwing begonias, and *B.schmidtiana*, *B.acaulis*, *B.acida* and trailing maroon hollyleaf *B.cubensis* species bloom well for me.

Some rhizomatous sorts, including the popular *B.bowerae* (the eyelash begonia), 'Maphil' ('Cleopatra'), 'Gaystar', and the winter-blooming tuberous begonias often fail to bloom unless given 12–14-hour nights. If you want maximum bloom on winter- to early-spring-blooming begonias, begin reducing day-length by half an hour each week starting in October. When your light garden provides 12–14-hour nights for four to eight weeks in the fall-winter season, many begonias will form flowers. Once blooming begins, gradually increase day-length so other types will remain in bloom.

Begonia goegoensis from Sumatra is a compact species for a warm, humid light garden.

Soil

The Basic Mix grows fine begonias in my collection. Soilfree formulas and Black Magic mix are also suitable, as is unmilled sphagnum moss with frequent applications of dilute fertilizer (see Chapter 9).

Growth Styles

Begonias are grouped according to their rooting habits and growth patterns, as Fibrous-rooted types, including the semperflorens hybrids; Rhizomatous with stems sprouting from above-ground rhizomes (as in the rex hybrids and *B. bowerae*); Tuberous-rooted types which are dormant for several months each year and a relatively new group; Rieger elatior hybrids which have fibrous roots and swollen semituberous stems at soil

Light soil mixes are perfect for begonias. This is a clump of plantlets produced from 'Gay Star', ready for a 2½-inch pot.

Begonia masoniana, a compact selection for warm light gardens.

Begonia 'Tom Ment'.

level. Hirsute types are known for hairy foliage. I identify some begonias as trailers, suitable to grow between other plants in the light garden or in baskets at windows, illuminated at night by reflector spots, or in locations where stems receive fluorescent light from all sides, not just above.

Fibrous-Rooted

Cane-stemmed angelwing hybrids are easy to grow 4–8 inches below tubes, but they must be frequently pinched and pruned to keep them under one foot. 'Tom Ment' is naturally dwarf and has lovely silver spotted foliage, pink flowers. 'Pinafore' is another outstanding compact type with silver spotted leaves, red below, salmon flowers.

Semperflorens hybrids require strong light, 4–6 inches under lamps for best flowering. Select naturally compact hybrids such as 'Ballet' with bronze leaves and double white flowers, or the dwarf-bedder selections easily raised from seed such as the 8-inch Galaxy bronze-leafed hybrids. For huge 2½–3-inch flowers in white, red, or pink, grow the 10–12-inch tall Butterfly hybrids.

Begonia acida, grown under Wide-Spectrum Gro-Lux.

Other fibrous-rooted gems to grow 4–8 inches under lamps include:

B.*acida*, slow creeper, 3–4 inches tall, round, dark-green pebbled leaves, constant display of white flowers on 6-inch spikes.

B.*aucalis* from New Guinea has thin light-green leaves and spires of true-pink flowers with yellow centers; it is fine in a terrarium or grown in unmilled sphagnum moss.

'Muriel Gray' is an exciting silver-and-coral-leafed hybrid of low-growing B.*pustulata* X B.*conchifolia*. You will find new hybrid selections in catalogues of such specialists as Kartuz, Logee's, and Merry Gardens (see Chapter 21).

Rhizomatous Selections

Appropriate in smaller light gardens are miniature and dwarf hybrids of B.*bowerae*, called the eyelash begonia for its fine hairs along the leaf edges. B.*bowerae nigramarga* grows 3–4 inches tall, has airy spires of white flowers. 'China Doll' is a good miniature with two-toned green leaves, pink flowers. 'Gaystar' is larger, to 8 inches tall and 12 inches across when established; stems and foliage are covered with fine green-silver hairs, the black-and-green leaves are star-shaped, the flowers pink. B.*prismatocarpa* is a yellow-flowered, 3–5-inch plant with plain green leaves, best in a terrarium. 'Red Planet' has glossy, round red leaves with a marbled pattern and a compact habit.

Rex Begonias

The rexes have brilliant foliage, often with a metallic glow. Thick rhizomes may lose most of their leaves if plants are kept below 60°, but under warm humid conditions most cultivars

Rex *Begonia* 'Merry Christmas', a vigorous clone.

Begonia pusulata (left) is one parent of *B.* 'Muriel Gray' (right) when crossed with *B.conchifolia*.

are lovely all year long. For a constant supply of **vigorous young** plants, root leaves every twelve to fifteen months. Keep rexes 6–8 inches from lamps for compact growth, but move them as far away as 15 inches if foliage seems weak colored. Grow an assortment from seed or try 'Merry Christmas' (red, green, silver), 'Shirt Sleeves,' (pink, silver, maroon), and 'It', a dwarf with silver leaves, pink flowers.

Trailing Begonias

Begonia cubensis. (6″–8″) Called the Hollyleaf begonia for its shiny maroon foliage. My plants constantly produce clusters of white flowers.

B.foliosa. (8″–12″) Tiny, almost fernlike, red-toned leaves, restrained growth.

B.pustulata. (8″–12″) Reminds me of thick carpet pile, **dark**-green flecked silver; it will ramble and root in perlite-fill**ed** trays.

B.solanthera. (6″–8″) Waxy, plain green foliage, clusters of fragrant white flowers, best in a raised pot or basket.

Tuberous Begonias

The large-flowered tuberous begonias, so lovely where summers are not too hot, bloom with long days but require short 10–12-hour days just before going dormant. Without the short days (long nights) they won't form underground tubers to sustain them during the required resting period. 'Switzerland' is a compact, red-flowered hybrid with bronze leaves; it did well for me under broad-spectrum lamps. Potted tuberous hybrids grown outdoors for summer decoration can be kept in bloom indoors through the fall by giving them 16 hours of light.

The tuberous *Begonia* 'Switzerland', single male flower of dark red with yellow pollen in the center. Leaves are bronze.

Rieger Cultivars

Rieger begonias are vigorous, large-flowered, elatior or winter-flowering semi-tuberous hybrids developed by Otto Rieger of Germany. Mr. Rieger first introduced the series in the late 1950's and early 1960's. Since that time they have won numerous medals and awards for horticultural excellence.

Among the dozen or so Riegers that I grow under various combinations of lamps, I have a few favorites for their abundance of flowers and superior response to light culture. 'Aphrodite Pink', like all the Aphrodite series, is a semitrailer, lovely in baskets, with fluffy double-pink flowers for months on end. 'Improved Schwabenland Orange' is a bushy upright grower with single orange flowers. 'Bernsteins Gelbe' is a 6–8-

inch bushy selection with clusters of light golden flowers blushed pink on the reverse.

Sources

Rieger cultivars are protected by trademarks and Plant Patents under a licensing system that pays royalties to the originators. In the United States Riegers are commercially propagated by Mikkelsens Inc. in Ohio, a firm well known for their superior poinsettias. Local growers and florists obtain small plants from Mikkelsens and usually offer them around winter and spring holidays when the Riegers are in full bloom.

Culture

Grow in the Basic Soil Mix or similar formula based on perlite and sphagnum peat. I potted some 'Schwabenland Red' plants in pure perlite and fertilized them with one-quarter-strength watersoluble 15–30–15 at nearly every watering. The plants flowered marvelously.

Pot in 4–6-inch containers with stem bases half an inch above the soil. To prevent powdery mildew, a main problem with this type of begonia, keep plants well spaced, not touching, and maintain good air circulation. A drench of Benlate and Dexon is used by commercial growers to protect Riegers from root rot and mildew, but with adequate room and an airy situation you may be able to avoid these troubles without the chemicals. If powdery mildew becomes a problem, apply Karathane fungicide, mixed 1/2 teaspoon per gallon of water. According to Mikkelsens the largest commercial grower of Rieger begonias, plain sulfur spray or dust is also effective against mildew. I find Aphrodite Riegers less likely to suffer from mildew than Schwabenland varieties.

Watering and Fertilizer

Water only after the soil has begun to dry. Apply lukewarm water during morning hours, either on the soil or from below. Always avoid wetting foliage. This type of begonia sheds water through leaf pores at night (guttation), which is why mildew can be a problem if humidity is high, plants are too close, or leaves get wet.

Avoid heavy applications of fertilizer that encourage foliage rather than bloom. For established Riegers in 5–6-inch pots it is safe to apply one half teaspoon of Osmocote or 3–M Precise slow-release fertilizer.

Temperature and Light

Best growth is made with night temperatures 70°–72° and a 14-hour day. When plants are full and well established, you will encourage bud formation by lowering temperatures to 65° at night and giving only 12 hours of light until flowering begins. A relative humidity of 40–50 percent is adequate.

After Flowering

When flowering is over, usually after several months, you can restore the then leggy plants by this procedure:

1. Gradually cut down on watering over a period of a week to dry out the juicy stems.
2. With a sharp razor or very keen knife cut off all of the heavy main stems to within 3 inches of the crown or base.
3. Keep the soil slightly dry as stem-cuts heal.
4. About one week after the pruning, shift the plant into a

container 1–2 inches larger than before. Keep the soil ball one-half inch above the new soil line.

5. Gradually resume watering, provide good light 4–6 inches under lamps, and in three to four months you will have a bushy flowering plant again.

I have success renewing Riegers from tip cuttings, but they also grow from sturdy middle-aged leaves.

Hirsute Types

Hairy-leafed selections endure humidity down to 40 percent, do best with slight drying at the roots between watering. Lovely selections are 'Priscilla Beck' (*B.* 'Brooks' X *B. venosa*) with succulent, red-blushed foliage; *B. leptotricha* 'Woolly Bear', a dwarf with brown plush stems and leaves; 'San Miguel', with an olive-green leaf, white frosting, red below, a parchment covering on stems; *B. schmidtiana*, a white-flowered dwarf.

16

Cacti and Other Succulents

The last time I walked through dusty Olduvai Gorge in Tanzania, I saw hundreds of succulent *Sansevieria ehrenbergii* growing among the thorn trees and rocks in full East African sun. It did not seem reasonable that these drought-resistant succulents would grow in captivity under lights, but seedlings of these same Tanzanian plants now thrive in my collection under broad-spectrum lumps.

Sunlight vs. Fluorescents

Cactus species from South America deserts and aloes from South Africa, which prosper with strong sun in their tropical to semitropical habitats, can with careful potting, restrained watering, and bright fluorescent lights live without sunlight in captivity. Some succulents look more beautiful when grown under artificial light than siblings living in a bright window. Uniform illumination and a succession of bright light-hours help succulents form symmetrical growth.

With less than optimum intensity or with light that fails to provide all the required colors (spectrum), succulents may change appearance. A glaucous or white-dusted species may be

Assorted succulents, mainly *Euphorbia* selections, thrive in the light garden of Ruth Gravelin's New York apartment under 14 hours of Vita-Lite illumination.

deep green or a short species grow tall and rangy. Such plants may be oddly attractive, presenting a new decorative aspect not revealed when the same species are grown under strong broad-spectrum light or in full sun.

Intensity

Succulents are genetically adapted to dryness and bright light. Some cacti, agaves, and similar desert species may live without rain for months. Other succulents, like aloes, haworthias, jungle cacti, crassulas, and stapelias, come from regions where they receive somewhat more moisture, usually from dew. These non-desert succulents are adapted to living with less than full sun. They thrive as epiphytes in the crotches of trees (jungle cactus), in tall grass or under thorny shrubs (aloes, haworthias), and in captivity need less light intensity than spiny desert cactus.

Grow succulents under broad-spectrum lamps, such as Agro-Lite, Wide-Spectrum Gro-Lux, and Vita-Lite. Keep foliage 3 to 6 inches below lamps, desert cactus plants directly under the center, other succulents at the ends. Or fill in the last one-quarter of your light garden at both ends with species that require the least light. Sansevierias, for example, can make healthy growth under lower light intensity than most other succulents.

A minimum humidity of 30 to 40 percent is sufficient.

Light-Hours

Provide intermediate to long days for a mixed succulent collection. In the fall begin to reduce day-length so that by winter you are growing succulents under 11-to-12-hour days.

Haworthia papillosa, a succulent for medium-light intensity, may form plantlets on old flower spikes.

Keep days short for eight weeks, then begin to lengthen light hours about one-half hour per week until plants receive 14-to-16-hour days. This routine permits a brief rest period and gives long-night species, such as kalanchoes, an opportunity to initiate flower buds.

Soils, Pots, and Fertilizers

Cacti, agaves, and most of the popular succulents thrive in the Basic Soil Mix, when 50 percent builders' coarse sand is added and pots have quick drainage. Or you may use a pasteurized mixture, a "Cactus Soil" sold in plastic bags at garden stores. An ideal mix for cacti and other succulents combines equal parts of oakleaf mold, coarse sand, and loam. These three ingredients are offered pre-pasteurized at garden stores.

Clay pots are fine for tall succulents that tend to topple if grown in lightweight plastic containers. Use a pot half as deep as the plant height. Unglazed clay will evaporate water and is therefore best for desert cactus and other species that need to dry out a little between watering. Mulch the base of succulents with gravel or stone chips. Light-colored stones reflect light into the plants and furnish a pleasant background to show off symmetrical shapes.

When succulents are making new growth, apply a one-quarter to one-half strength fertilizer solution at every other watering. Use a balanced formula or one with slightly less nitrogen than phosphorus and potash.

In Summer

When your conditions permit, transfer succulents to a bright location outdoors in June. Let them grow in sun until September. But even desert cactus should be exposed gradually since strong fluorescent light is still weaker than direct hot

I found this cold-hardy cactus (*Soehrensia bruchii* syn. *Lobivia*) near Portillo, Chile, with snow all around. Many cacti tolerate low night temperatures and are ideal for light gardens in unheated areas. (Joaquin Toledo photo)

summer sun. Summer growth in sunlight is especially important for desert species.

Kinds to Grow

Select miniature and compact succulents for small light gardens. Large specimens are dramatic but difficult to light evenly. For specimen plants next to bright windows, consider using reflector incandescents for dramatic night lighting and to supplement daylight on sunless days. The most rewarding success under fluorescents comes with succulents that grow in less than full sun in their native habitats.

Succulents Other Than Desert Cacti

Adromischus. (4″–6″) South African dwarfs resembling spotted birds eggs. Attractive are *A.cooperi, A.festivus, A.maculatus.*

Agave. (3″–4″) Spiny-leaved New World counterparts to the African aloes but tougher, with spine-tipped leaves on most species. Try compact *A.filifera compacta, A.striata nana, A.victoriae-reginae.*

Miniature aloes are lovely under lights. Top row, left to right, *Aloe variegata, Haworthia fasciata, Aloe rauhii.* Center, *Aloe bellatula, A.haworthiodes.* Bottom, left to right, *Aloe praetense. A.jacunda.*

Aloe. (4″–8″) Undemanding miniatures include *A.brevifolia depressa*, *A.haworthioides*, *A.humilis*. Grow *A.vera* to treat burns.

Crassula. (4″–6″) Most famous is the jadeplant, *C.argentea*, a slow-growing delight with thick round leaves, nice as a bonsai tree. Other rewarding compact sorts include *C.coperi* with half-inch, gray-green leaves on trailing stems and many white flowers; *C.perforata* stems resemble a pagoda tower; *C.lycopodioides* has braided strap stems; *C.schmidtii* is a low creeper with a long blooming season when it is covered with deep-pink flowers.

Echeveria. (4″–6″) Rosettes resemble those of the cold-hardy sempervivums, but echeverias are from Mexico. Delightful, easy-to-care-for species with metallic tones are the compact *E.derenbergii*, *E.elegans*, *E.pulvinata* (fuzzy foliage).

Edithcolea grandis. (3″–4″) This East African creeper resembles stapelia, bright yellow and maroon flowers.

Edithcolea grandis photographed in Tsavo, Kenya.

199

Euphorbia. (4"–8") A genus of drastically different species classified on the basis of flower form rather than plant habit. The Christmas poinsettia is *E.pulcherrima.* Best under lights are *E.Keysii*, a continually flowering hybrid crown-of-thorns with pink flowers. Prune in summer to keep plants under 12 inches. *E.lactea* has thick, green, stumpy stems marked cream and short black thorns. The distorted *E.cristata* is a compact 4 to 8 inches. *E.splendens*, the classic crown-of-thorns, is most manageable in the dwarf 'Bojeri' form (deep red) and there is an unnamed, new yellow-flowered long-leafed cultivar. These bloom even with short nights.

Faucaria. (3"–6") The tiger-jaws get their popular name from soft, tooth-shaped hairs along the fleshy leaf margins. Attractive and compact are *F.tigrina* and *F.tuberculosa.*

xGasterhaworthia. (*Gasteria* X *Haworthia*) (4"–8") 'Royal Highness' is a compact symmetrical hybrid with dark foliage dotted white.

Gasteria. (4"–6") Thick tongue-shaped leaves grow from the center, forming a narrow upright plant. *G.verrucosa* from South Africa is interesting for white "warts" on tough foliage.

xGastrolea. (*Gasteria* X *Aloe*) (4"–8") 'Spotted Beauty' grows in a rosette that resembles the aloe parent but the texture and substance is like that of gasteria. An adaptable bronze-blushed gem for light gardens.

Haworthia. (4"–8") The group photo gives an idea of several attractive compact species. Haworthias may burn in full sun but respond to strong fluorescent light with compact growth. This is an excellent genus for your light garden. *H.fasciata* and the similar but smaller (2 to 3 inches)

Haworthia cultivars grown under artificial light.

H.subfasciata are delightfully symmetrical and full. Dark green leaves, wide at the base, come to a point but without a dangerous spine. Decorative raised-white bands inspire the popular name zebra haworthia. *H.papillosa* is a 2-to-4-inch dwarf with white dots all over the foliage. Most haworthias produce small green or coral-orange flowers on thin stems.

Hoodia. (3″–4″) Gray-green columnar stems, short soft spines, round brownish pink or maroon flowers.

Kalanchoe. (4″–8″) The hybrid yellow-and-red *K.blossfeldiana* selections, so popular during the winter holidays, do well under lights. Seed sown in the spring is grown until fall with 16–18-hour days. In late September night-length should be increased until the mature plants have 13–14 hours of darkness per 24-hour period (completely uninterrupted) to initiate flower buds. After three months of long nights, flowers will open and the night-length can be shortened if you wish. Use tip cuttings to carry over select clones from year to year. *K.pinnata* (syn. *Bryophyllum*) is called air plant for its habit of producing plantlets along leaf margins, as does the more attractive

Kalanchoe tubiflora (left) and *K. daigremontiana* (right) form plantlets on mature leaves.

K.daigremontiana and round-leafed *K.tubiflora*. *K.tomentosa* or teddy-bear has compact stems, thick silver-plush leaves marked dark brown along the edges. Kalanchoes are propagated from leaves, seeds and tip cuttings.

Pachyphytum. (3″-4″) These Mexican plants resemble glaucous gray or silver sedums, often with leaf tips blushed rose. Lovely under lights, slow growing.

Portulaca. (2″-4″) Trailing annuals with bright 1-inch flowers in white, orange, red, pink. Try the dwarf 'Tuffet', a hybrid that makes a 4-inch blooming clump.

Portulacaria. (4″-6″) A delightful 3-to-6-inch dwarf resembling a small tree is *P.afra-variegata* from South Africa. Ideal in tiny landscapes. Foliage is marked cream and rose.

Sansevieria. (6″-10″) The snake-plants are true succulents but are very tolerant of low light. They do best when the soil is kept lightly moist, not soggy. A good 3-to-6-inch dwarf is *S.trifasciata hahnii*, available with silver or gold leaf markings.

Sedum. (2″-6″) Species from warm areas of the world do well indoors. Propagation is quick from individual leaves, which root at the base. *S.morganianum*, the burrotail, has glaucous silver leaves on trailing stems, hanging straight if the pot is raised. *S.multiceps* is treelike, fun for a land-scaped succulent garden. *S.pachyphyllum*, called jelly beans, has fat, silver-green leaves blushed rose, an easy-to-manage clump of growth.

Senecio. (3″-4″) A slow, compact trailing species is *S.herreianus* with the perfect common name of marble-vine; it looks like a necklace of green pearls. *S.macroglossus variegatus* resembles a waxy variegated ivy, but it is much more tolerant of low humidity than true ivy.

Stapelia. (4″-8″) The stapelias I found in Rhodesia and Tanzania were growing with partial shade on sandy ground. In captivity these starfish-plants thrive with even moisture while in active growth. Grow in shallow pots so stems can trail and root where they touch soil. Flowers on some species smell like rotten meat which has earned them the name of carrion-flower, but the scent is not overpowering unless you put your nose right into the big 10- to12-inch flowers. The largest clump of *S.gigantea* I have seen in captivity was growing in a biology classroom under two 40-watt Gro-Lux tubes. The fleshy green stems, 6 to 8 inches tall, were covered with buds and flowers and filled half of the light-cart shelf. More compact are *S.hirsuta*, 3 to 8 inches tall with hairy cream-and-maroon flowers, *S.semota lutea* (yellow), and *S.variegata*, 2 to 4 inches tall with gray-green stems and yellow 2- to 3-inch flowers heavily marked purple, all excellent under lights.

Cacti

The true cacti are succulents, but they often have spines, flowers spring directly from the stems, and many of the desert species will endure very strong light. It is practical to divide cacti into two major groups: the *desert* cacti, which come from dry regions in the semitropical to tropical areas, and the *jungle* cacti, which are found in the more moist, high-altitude locations of Central and South America.

Desert Cacti (2"-4")

Intense light is required for desert cactus to make normal growth. Grow them in full sun during the warm months, then place them 2 to 4 inches below broad-spectrum lamps in winter. If you can't put them outside in summer, then continue to maintain them under strong fluorescents, with good air circulation and somewhat damper soil while they are making new growth. Little water is required when plants are not growing, usually during winter rests.

Pot desert cacti in small containers using sharp drainage of pebbles or crock with some hardwood charcoal added. The soil mixture should be gritty and quick draining. These cacti endure low humidity; they will also accept cool nights, down to the 40's, especially in winter. Cool nights encourage blooming.

Extend the show period by growing species with unusual shapes or colorful spines, interesting even when plants are without flowers. Both species and hybrids are suitable and will be seen in the specialists' catalogues listed in Chapter 21.

Chamaecereus silvestrii, the peanut-cactus, forms a clump of cylindrical stems covered with delicate spines; then 2- to 3-inch red flowers appear in spring.

Paramount hybrid 'Pink and White' is a miniature.

Echinocactus grusonii, the golden-barrel of Mexico has brilliant yellow spines. Nice as a seedling under lights, it eventually forms a 24- to 30-inch dome.

Mammillaria bocasana, the Mexican healthy-mouth cactus looks like a 1- to 3-inch ball of cotton. *M.elongata*, also from Mexico, develops a low cluster of finger-sized stems covered with yellow spines. The pale yellow to white flowers appear in early spring.

Opuntia microdasys is grown for the clumps of flat pads, dotted all over with soft yellow spines (glochids).

Paramount hybrids are a modern group of dwarf 3- to 5-inch cacti forming clusters of spiny domes; these are available in clones with red, yellow, orange, or pink flowers. (*Echinopsis* X *Lobivia* X *Chamaecerus*).

Parodia aureispina forms a 2- to 3-inch globe decorated with yellow spines.

Rebutia species are tiny 1- to 2-inch spiny balls, at home in 2-inch pots or miniature landscapes.

Grafted "Bunnies"

Yellow, red, pink, or orange mutations of *Gymnocalycium* are often offered grafted onto vigorous plain green rootstocks. These odd cactus creations provide year-round color. Even stranger are normal cactus such as *Notocactus* species or *Espostoa lanata* (the old-man) grafted on the top of plain green stems. These look top heavy but grow well under intense broad-spectrum light or a combination of sunlight and fluorescents.

Jungle Cacti (4"–10")

Unlike their desert relatives, jungle cacti do not require strong light. In fact direct sun may burn the fleshy green pads. However they seldom burn under fluorescents and thrive with bright artificial light. They require 50–60 percent humidity.

Best known are the Thanksgiving and Christmas cactus. In the tropics I find these with orchids and bromeliads growing in tree crotches where their roots are protected by moss or rotting leaves. Drainage is sharp but night dews and occasional heavy rains keep the plants plump. Temperatures fall into the 50's at night but in captivity a drop into the low 60's is sufficient.

Another popular jungle group are called orchid-cactus, after the wide 6- to 8-inch flowers. Hybrids of these *Epiphyllum* cultivars are available in a dazzling multitude of colors. The arching or trailing stems grow 1- to 2-feet long and so are not as practical under lights as the Christmas cactus.

Soil

Pot in soil with a high humus content but quick drainage. The Basic Soil Mix (Chapter 9), with added leaf mold and sharp sand is excellent. Black Magic planter-mix, combined with 25 percent medium orchid potting bark (redwood or fir) and 25 percent coarse sand, is another fine formula for the jungle-cactus group. These grow best with even moisture at the roots, but when they are resting in winter let them dry out slightly between waterings.

Night Hours

Christmas and Thanksgiving cactus are sensitive to both night-length and temperature. At 60°–65°, they set flower buds during nights of 13–14 hours. When night temperatures drop to 50° plants bloom even with short nights. When the dark hours are warm (68°–75°), they fail to set flower buds, regardless of night-length.

For maximum bloom be sure plants have 13- to 14-hour nights from late September into December. The usual 60°–65° night temperatures, combined with the long nights, will let plants set flower buds. If you put your jungle cactus outside for the summer, let them stay out until just before frost. This will help them bloom abundantly.

Propagation

Propagate the jungle cacti from tip cuttings set in moist sand or in a perlite-milled sphagnum moss mixture.

Thanksgiving (*Zygocactus*) and Christmas (*Schlumbergera*) are available in pink, red, orange, or white. I have a shallow clay pot planted with white (*Zygocactus truncatus delicatus*) and orange Thanksgiving hybrids. They make a delightful color combination from October to November, and again in March.

Epiphyllums come in many different colors. Send for the specialists' catalogues (Chapter 21) and select those that are most appealing to you. A vigorous dwarf red is 'Elegantissimum'.

Rhipsalis, the mistletoe cactus, is an excellent genus to grow under lights. The thick green stems and fat noddle-shaped leaves are often covered with hairs but never harmful spines. Small white or yellow flowers are followed by lasting berries. I have seen rhipsalis growing in the jungle as an epiphyte next to orchids, ferns, peperomias, and bromeliads. Some nice species include: *R.mesembryanthemoides* with white flowers and creamy berries and *R.quellenbambensis* with red berries.

Pseudoripsalis macrantha resembles a narrow-stemmed Christmas cactus, but it has starry fragrant white flowers. My plant has been in the same 3-inch plastic pot for four years and is doing well, with branching stems now 8 to 9 inches long.

17
International Flowers —
Tender and Hardy Bulbs

Rewarding flowering plants for indoor light gardens are found in species from all over the world. Sometimes a genus has but one or two species suitable for houseplants, but these deserve mention for their unique characteristics. The following plants with delightful flowers in unique forms will give an international air to your light garden.

Agapanthus 'Peter Pan'. (6″–8″) A dwarf blue-flowered Lily-of-the-Nile, 12- to 15-inches tall, with thick nearly bulbous roots and strap foliage, forms a vigorous clump.

Anthurium. (8″–15″) *A.andraeanum* may reach 3 feet. If you have the space, it will thrive indoors with warm humid conditions. Waxy spathes in white, pink, or red last a month or more. The compact 10- to 15-inch *A.scherzerianum*, the flamingo or pigtail anthurium, is better suited to modest-sized gardens. The standard variety is orange-red with a yellow twisted spadix on which appear the minute flowers. Variety 'Rothschildianum' is white with red spots, 'Album' is white.

WS GRO-LUX VITA-LITE GRO-LUX

Allophyton mexicanum, grown from seed under three different fluorescent light sources. Wide-Spectrum Gro-Lux produced the largest most floriferous plants, standard Gro-Lux plants bloomed several weeks after plants under the other two lamps.

Allophyton mexicanum. (4″–6″) The Mexican foxglove is an everblooming compact gem with waxy, dark green foliage and 4–6-inch stalks of lavender flowers. Easy from seed.

Aphelandra squarrosa. (6″–8″) The zebra-plant has shiny, deep green leaves prominantly veined white and a spectacular yellow inflorescence when given 10-to-12-hour days in the fall. Cultivar 'Dania' is compact.

Beloperone guttata. (4″–6″) The shrimp-plant is nearly always in bloom with yellow or red-toned bracts, more colorful than the small white flowers they surround.

Bougainvillea. (3″–6″) (broad-spectrum lamps) These vigorous vines will bloom if kept close to broad-spectrum lamps or given some sun each day. Train along a wire, or prune into a bushy shrub. Hybrids are available in white, pink, orange, and magenta.

Capsicum annuum conoides. (3″–6″) The Christmas-pepper is an easy annual from seed, soon forming a 6-to-10-inch

Christmas peppers (*Capsicum annuum conoides*) grown from seed under fluorescent lamps. Fruit turns red as it ripens.

Calamondin orange [Citrus mitis) has fragrant flowers and fruit forming during most of the year.

clump of foliage topped with white flowers, then with tiny peppers that begin yellow, soon turn red. They can be eaten but are hot. Grow new plants from seed after fruit falls.

Citrus shrubs. (4″-6″) Dwarf citrus trees need 1- to 2-square feet of space but produce a constant succession of fragrant flowers followed by bright fruit. Mist foliage to discourage red spider mites. Cool nights encourage compact growth.

Crossandra infundibuliformis. (4″-6″) Glossy, dark-green foliage, orange flowers from a pagoda-shaped spike, on and off all year long. From seeds or cuttings.

Exacum affine. (4″-8″) The German-violets bloom in four to five months from seed, produce bushy 6- to 10-inch plants covered with round violet-blue, fragrant flowers. Seedlings of 'Midget' hybrids under Verilux and Wide-Spectrum Gro-Lux bloomed before siblings in my greenhouse. Sow seed on top of milled sphagnum moss.

Exacum affine 'Midget' grown from seed had largest plants, most flowers under Wide-Spectrum Gro-Lux. Mature plants continued to bloom freely 3 inches under a 50/50 combination of Cool White and Warm White.

Hoya. (3″-6″) The wax-vines are slow-growing Australian and Malasian trailers with thick succulent foliage and clusters of waxy, fragrant flowers, best trained on a support. Growth stops for several months in winter, even under lights. When this occurs reduce watering, stop fertilizer. Most adaptable are *H.carnosa* cultivars, such as 'Crimson King' and 'Exotica' with white and rose-blushed foliage. *H.bella* has thinner stems, smaller leaves, more graceful growth but can be reluctant bloomer. *H.lacunosa* is a charming miniature.

Impatiens. (6″-8″) New dwarf impatiens hybrids, created for outdoor bedding, bloom for months on 12-to-14-hour

Hoya carnosa 'Exotica' with seed pod and fragrant flowers.

days. 'Scarlet Ripple', a bright red with white markings, makes a 4- to 8-inch mound. Exciting hybrids created from New Guinea species have colorful foliage to compliment orange, pink, or magenta flowers. On the Cyclone hybrids, derived from New Guinea impatiens, foliage color is most brilliant with long days, flowers most abundant with 12-hour days, 12-hour nights. An excellent cultivar is 'Star Fire', a bright orange flower against yellow-centered leaves. 'Blue Velvet' has purple flowers on a bushy plant with satin-textured red-veined foliage. Among the dwarf, plain-leaved hybrids 'Elfin' impatiens are rewarding under lights. Propagate impatiens from tip cuttings or seed sown on top of milled sphagnum moss. Germination occurs at 65° to 70° about 6 inches under lamps. Light encourages even germination. All impatiens do best in the well-drained Standard Mix (Chapter 9) or similar peat-like formulas with a constant supply of balanced fertilizer.

Ixora. (4"–6") Bright balls or red or orange flowers during colder months earn space for ixora shrubs. *I.coccinea* has glossy foliage, red flowers. *I.javanica* has salmon-red flowers. Prune for compact growth since natural height for these shrubs outdoors is 4 to 5 feet!

Jasminum. (6"–8") White flowers with heavy perfume are the main feature of jasmine-vines. With careful trimming they will form a bushy shrub. *J.sambac* 'Grand Duke', an Arabian cultivar, produces double flowers throughout the year. *J.nitidum* (*J.gracile magnificum*) is more of a vine, has starry flowers in winter. Jasmines tolerate nights into the low 50's. Provide 12- to 14-hour nights late fall into winter.

Malpighia coccigera. (6"–8") Glossy prickly holly-form foliage and lacy light pink flowers characterize this charming shrublet, which is nice for a bonsai. Propagate from half-ripe tip cuttings.

Oxalis regnellii from South America.

Oxalis regnellii. (4″–8″) This provides a constant succession of white flowers on 4- to 6-inch stalks above clover-shaped foliage, which is blushed maroon underneath. Keep evenly moist. This must be groomed of dead lower leaves and spent flowers or it soon looks bedraggled.

Punica granatum nana. (4″–8″) The dwarf pomegranate thrives for me under Gro-Lux or Wide-Spectrum Gro-Lux tubes, producing a succession of brilliant orange flowers spring into winter. It is best when given a cool rest for six to eight weeks in winter if growth stops and foliage falls. Pinch during growing season to make a bushy shrub. Pollinate flowers for edible fruit. Plants I grew from seed bloomed in ten months grown with 14-hour days.

Rhoeo spathacea (syn. *R.discolor*). (6″–8″) This low rosette of olive-green foliage, marked maroon below, is called Moses-in-the-boat for the tiny white flowers which appear in boat-shaped cups at the base of sword-shaped leaves. Slow from seed but tip cuttings root well in water, and cuttings are an excellent way to shorten older plants that develop 6- to 8-inch bare stems after several years.

Roses. (4″-6″) Miniature roses thrive with broad-spectrum light, and daytime temperatures around 75°, nights into the low 60's, 14-to-16-hour days, evenly moist roots. Tiny flowers are often fragrant and make charming miniature arrangements. Cut blooms with long stems to make compact plants and to encourage the new growth on which flowers are produced. Even if you don't cut flowers for decoration, still prune back branches after flowers fade, or plants will get too tall. Cut stems about halfway back.

After miniature roses produce flowers for nine to ten months under lights, encourage a cool four- to six-week resting period, with nights into the 40's. I do this by leaving plants outside in the fall, bringing them inside around Christmas. Just before bringing them in, prune away dead branches, cut back up to three quarters of top growth, repot in fresh soil (Standard Mix), and spray with a combination of Benlate and Isotox to protect against insects and fungus.

Miniature roses are cold-hardy wherever the larger hybrid teas thrive, so there is no danger that they will die if left outside until cold weather, but do mulch them if they are to stay outdoors all winter long. Famous rose breeder Harm Saville told me that some miniatures are able to indicate whether or not the artificial light is adequate in strength and spectrum. Harm reports that he uses 'Willie Mae' as a light quality-quantity indicator, since the blooms will be medium red with adequate light but get increasingly lighter, almost pink, with poor light. I found this to be true of 'Willie Mae' in my own tests. Send for color illustrated catalogues of miniature rose specialists listed in Chapter 21; then pick for favorite colors.

Spathiphyllum. (6″–10″) The sword-shaped, deep green leaves of spathiphyllums make them attractive all year, but I enjoy these South American aroids for their long-lasting white flowers (spathes) which have a subtle perfume. 'Mauna Loa' looks like a white anthurium with 4- to 5-inch white spathes. *S.clevelandii* (syn. *S.patinii*) is an 8- to 12-inch cultivar, excellent under lights. Keep soil evenly moist but well drained.

Stephanotis floribunda. (4″–6″) The Madagascar jasmine-vine succeeds under lights but must be trained on a trellis. Thick, glossy, evergreen leaves 3 to 4 inches long provide a pleasing background for clusters of 2-inch white, fragrant flowers. Keep drier at roots during winter months when no new leaves are being produced.

Tropaeolum tricolor. (4″–6″) This is a dainty climbing nasturtium with divided leaves and a multitude of 1-inch brilliant red, tubular flowers, each marked purple-and-yellow at the lip. I found this growing in its native Chile scrambling over low shrubs. Under lights give it a trellis up to 12-inches square. It is grown from small bulblets or seed, and usually goes dormant in our North American summer.

Bulbs

Tender bulbs and warm-growing tuberous plants, usually sold as bulbs, thrive under fluorescents with little more than careful potting and watering. Most have a dormant period during which they should be rested in their pots with much less water. No light is required for dormant bulbs or tubers. Repotting is done just as dormant bulbs begin new growth.

Amaryllis hybrid.

After Blooming

Success with bulbs depends upon how you care for the plants after they bloom. Once flowers fade the bulbs begin to grow leaves to store energy for the next season's show. Keep them under good light, provide even moisture, and adequate fertilizer until leaves begin to fade.

Amaryllis. (4"–6") These striking winter- and spring-blooming bulbs are botanically hybrids in the genus *Hippeastrum* but they are sold as *Amaryllis* in America. I have raised hundreds of hybrids from seed, flowering most in three years when I give seedlings 16- to 18-hour days. Mature bulbs may grow 30 to 36 inches tall even though they are in 6-inch pots, so space must be provided. The best system is to grow bulbs outside during the warm months, let them go dormant in fall, then flower them under lights during cold months. Flats of seedlings, up to the fourth year, can be kept in constant growth whatever the location. If seedlings don't go dormant after the fourth summer, just withhold water to ripen the bulbs and encourage blooming.

Most compact are the *A.gracilis* cultivars with 10- to 15-inch scapes, easier to manage under lights than the taller 24- to 30-inch flower stalks of the standard hybrids. Begin growing amaryllis by purchasing a large bulb from a local or mailorder nursery. Small bulbs, although less expensive, may not bloom. Pot in Standard Mix with the top half of the bulb above ground. Place where temperatures are 70° to 75°. Slight bottom heat will speed rooting. Night temperatures 55° –60° are best after flowers have opened; coolness helps them to last longer.

Eucharis grandiflora. (6″–8″) Flowers of the fragrant, white, daffodil-shaped Amazon-lily appear several times each year under lights. Bulbs tolerate cool nights, do not require a dormant rest, but must become established before maximum blooming occurs. Repot every four to five years. The dark green shiny foliage resembles that of the aspidistra.

Eucomis. (4″-6″) The pineapple-lily has a bloom spike that springs from a rosette of medium-green leaves, giving the naked stalk and cluster of starry flowers a pineapple-plant profile. *E.bicolor* is the most compact, 12 to 15 inches tall; it thrives with intermediate to cool nights and the same culture as amaryllis.

Haemanthus. (4″–6″) The African blood-lilies produce balls of bright orange or fire-red flowers spring to fall. Culture as for amaryllis. *H.katherine*, a deep red, and *H.multiflorus*, coral-red, are 12- to 15-inch species suitable for light gardens.

Veltheimia. (6″–8″) You will have to give a square foot of space to this South African bulb but spikes of rose-coral flowers and a rosette of broad glossy foliage pay the rent. This accepts cool nights, has a 2- to 3-month dormant period during northern summers. *V.glauca* (syn. *V.*

capensis) 'Rosabla' is a white-and-rose flowered species, *V.viridiflora* the most often seen, has a 15- to 18-inch spike of deep-pink flowers from late winter into spring.

Zadescantia. (4″–6″) Calla lilies grow 12 to 24 inches tall; they bloom under lights if given moist humus-rich soil and bright broad-spectrum light. Most practical are *Z.elliottina* with soft golden-yellow flowers, lovely deep green leaves spotted silver, and the new hybrids with *Z.rehmannii*, which have pastel bronze, pink, and lavender-toned flowers and compact growth. All require a 2 to 3 month dormant period.

Hardy Bulbs

Cold-hardy bulbs will bloom in a light garden if given a ten to twelve week cool, dark, rooting period first. Most satisfactory are compact types such as crocus, muscari, and bulbous iris.

Selection

By late September you can obtain a nice selection at your local garden centers or look for them in mailorder catalogues (Chapter 21). Stores that offer Dutch bulbs have a free folder from the Netherlands Bulb Institute showing the steps for forcing bulbs indoors. The basic requirement is the cold, dark, rooting period. Select the largest bulbs you can find for maximum display. Small bulbs are never a bargain for indoor growing.

Potting

Put drainage gravel or crocks plus a few chunks of hardwood charcoal in the bottom of each clay or plastic three-quarter pot or bulb pan. Cover the drainage material with a one-half inch layer of unmilled sphagnum moss, then add the standard mix to within about 3 inches of the top. Set bulbs into the soil and almost touching each other, then add more soil mix and tap the pot on a hard surface to settle the soil. Let the top third of the bulbs protrude just above the surface. If you barely cover the bulbs they will then be slightly exposed after you water them in from above. Soak the potting mix.

Rooting Period

Place the pots in a dark place where temperatures stay above 32°; 40° to 50° is a good range. Suitable places for the rooting period include cool basements, attics, a garage where temperatures don't fall to freezing, or even a refrigerator set at 50°. In ten to twelve weeks if bulbs have produced good roots, set the pots 4 to 6 inches under fluorescent lamps, gradually moving the lamps higher as the bulbs send up flower spikes.

The only hardy bulbs that bloom well for me without the cool ten- to twelve-week rooting period are the autumn crocus and semihardy paperwhite narcissus.

Flowering Time

When flowers open you can place the pots anywhere you wish for display, but remember that cool nights will prolong bloom. Keep roots evenly moist. After flowers fade begin feeding with a water-soluble fertilizer if you want to put bulbs outdoors for garden decoration. Bulbs don't force well more than one year. Crocus, hyacinths, narcissus, tulips, and similar cold-hardy species will bloom in the garden after a year or two of indoor growing to regain their strength, but the tender narcissus may as well be discarded.

18

Bromeliads, the Durable Air Plants

Familiar bromeliads include the pineapple, a terrestrial plant famous for its juicy fruit, and Spanish moss (*Tillandsia usneoides*), a popular symbol of the Old South where it drapes cypress and oak trees. Durability is a primary characteristic of bromeliads. Most of the species develop foliage in a cup-shaped rosette, which holds water.

In the jungles I have collected bromeliads that harbored in their cups insect larvae, snakes, frogs, lizards, and scorpions! Wild bromeliads obtain their nourishment from rotting organic matter that accumulates in the rosettes. Only a few, such as the succulent dyckias and terrestrial pineapples, obtain much food from underground roots.

Culture

Epiphytic bromeliads, by far the largest number of species in captivity, have roots adapted for holding onto branches. These bromeliads do best in mixtures of bark and perlite, mounted on slabs of tree-fern or grown in sphagnum moss stuffed into cork holders or drilled-out tree branches. Potting in clay containers is usually the most convenient in light gardens.

Terrestrial species thrive in gritty humus-rich mixtures of peatmoss, perlite, and small bark chips. Bromeliads raised from seed will have more fibrous roots than jungle-collected plants, and it is more important to keep water in the rosette than to wet roots. Pot bromeliads in relatively small containers with excellent drainage. Even terrestrials do best when pots are sharply drained.

Light

I have good results with many species under broad-spectrum lamps. Mature plants bloom when given sufficient light intensity and 12- to 14-hour days. Those species with silvery scales (some *Tillandsias*, for example) require the brightest light with tubes 3 to 6 inches away, while those with thin leaves (*Vrieseas*, etc.) do well with medium-light intensity, the tubes 6 to 10 inches away. Under fluorescent lights bromeliads

Epiphytic bromeliads on mountain slopes in Guatemala.

can utilize fertilizer whenever they are growing. Apply a half-strength water-soluble balanced formula, alternated with fish emulsion, every month. Every 3 to 4 months wash out the rosettes and fill with fresh water. Bromeliads thrive outdoors during warm months.

To encourage winter flowering on species that normally bloom during the short days of November into January (*Billbergia nutans* for example), provide 12- to 13-hour nights from October to January.

Propagation

A number of showy species have grown well for me from seed sown on the 50/50 perlite and milled sphagnum moss mixture, started with bottom heat. Even the epiphytic species develop excellent root systems. Easiest from seed are *Aechmea* and *Billbergia*, but you must wait three to four years for flowers.

Vegetative propagation is faster than seeds. Small plantlets form alongside the older rosettes or from within the mature growth in vrieseas. Bromeliad rosettes die after flowering but this decline may take more than a year; during this time plantlets form to carry on. You can remove these offsets when they have some roots of their own. Pot them tightly in small clay pots, keep the center rosettes filled with water, guard against having the limited root system constantly wet.

The bushy *Tillandsia usenoides*, and other clumping species, can be gently pulled apart, the smaller sections then mounted on fern slabs. Mist these daily because the silvery tillandsias retain little water.

Selections to Grow

Aechmea. (3″–6″) Aechmeas endure low humidity, hold water in center rosettes, and are grown for foliage and flowers. *A.chantinii* needs a warm humid atmosphere; it has mottled foliage. *A.fasciata* is adaptable, even to dry interiors if the rosette is filled with water. Silvery scales decorate foliage and the inflorescence brings the height to

Aechmea hybrid *Maginalii* (*A.miniata* x *A.fulgens*) with long-lasting fruit forming.

15 to 20 inches. It has pink bracts, blue flowers for many weeks.

A.miniata var. *discolor* grows 10 to 18 inches tall; leaves are green on top, maroon underneath. Blue flowers are followed by long-lasting red berries.

Ananas comosus var. *variegatus.* (3″–6″) This pineapple is grown for its gold-edged leaves. For fruit select the dwarf *A.nanus*, which grows 12 to 15 inches tall and has small ornamental fruit.

Billbergia. (3″–6″) Rewarding species for foliage and flowers. *B.nutans*, called queens-tears is a rapid growing, slender tubular 8- to 15-inch plant with a cascading inflorescence of pink bracts and violet-blue flowers. *B.zebrina*, a Brazilian epiphyte, can reach 30 inches but is attractive even as a seedling for its cylinder of silver-banded leaves, blushed maroon in bright light.

225

Cryptanthus 'It', white, olive-green, and pink.

Crypthanthus. (4″-10″) The earth-stars are delightfully compact Brazilian species, appreciated for variegated foliage and leaves of various colors, sometimes resembling a snake skin. *C.bivittatus* forms a 2- to 3-inch rosette to 6 inches across. Foliage is striped red, pink, and cream, varying in tone according to light intensity. *C.fosterianus* is one of the larger species, reaching 20 to 30 inches across, with pink-brown rosettes crossed-barred with silver and dark brown. *C.zonatus* forms compact rosettes 4 to 8 inches across with foliage resembling reptile skin, patterned in wavy cross bars of silver and brown.

Guzmania. (6″-10″) The orange or red bracts that form a starry rosette around short-lived white flowers on guzmanias will last in beauty for months. Leaves form a low water-holding circle. *G.lingulata* and its cultivars are excellent under lights. This species comes from warm moist jungles in Central and South America where it grows as an epiphyte in trees, with roots protected by moss. In captivity pot it in a well-drained mix of perlite, leafmold, and sphagnum peatmoss or in one of the terrestrial orchid mixes, over at least an inch of gravel and hardwood charcoal. *G.lingulata* var. *cardinalis,* from the Colombian Andes, has brilliant red-orange bracts from a foliage rosette 12 to 15 inches across. 'Magnifica', offered in some catalogues, is a compact hybrid of *G.lingulata* var. *cardinalis* X *G.lingulata* var. *minor*.

Neoregelia. (6″–10″) These terrestrial or semiepiphytic jungle species, mostly from Brazil, are well worth growing for their colorful foliage. Small blue or white flowers open just above the water inside of the foliage cups. Most spectacular is *N.carolinae tricolor*, with green-and-white striped leaves, the centers turning vivid scarlet for 4 to 5 months.

Nidularium. (6″–10″) Nidulariums are named for their nest-shaped water-holding rosettes (from *nidus*, the Latin for nest), a perfect description for leaves forming a protective circle for tiny white or blue flowers which open just above the water. Grow nidulariums for maroon-and-green foliage. In their native Brazilian jungles, the species thrive in shaded places on trees, on moss-covered rocks, or in sharply-drained ground. Pot them in well-drained mixtures, as suggested for *Guzmania*, keep cups filled with water. Nidulariums thrive beside neoregelias, thin-leaved tillandsias, and vrieseas. *Nidularium innocentii* has dark maroon leaves; variety *lineatum* is white and green.

Tillandsia. (3″–6″ for silvery kinds. 6″–10″ for the thin green species). The silver-scaled species of *Tillandsia* are adapted to low humidity and strong light. They absorb water quickly through the glaucous foliage scales but hold little water in the foliage rosettes. In contrast, the thin-leaved green species need less intense light, require higher humidity, and hold water in their centers. Among the thin-leaved species with attractive upright flowering spikes are *T.cyanea* of Ecuador with 12- to 15-inch rosettes, and a light-pink inflorescence 4 to 6 inches high with bright blue flowers appearing over a period of weeks, and the similar *T.lindenii*. Compact silver-leaved species

I photographed these epiphytic silver-scaled tillandsias in an oak-pine forest of Guatemala.

to grow under lights include *T.ionantha*, a perfect 1- to 2-inch miniature, best grown on a slab of tree-fern, and *T.usneoides*, the Spanish moss, a perfect decoration for miniature fruit trees or to hang on branches of coffee shrubs. When the small blue flowers of *T.ionantha* appear, the center leaves turn scarlet. *T.usneoides* is grown for its silvery strands. Mist the silvery species daily, but let the roots dry a little between waterings.

Vriesea. (6″–10″) The flaming-swords are rather tall for growing under lights; the inflorescence can reach 2 feet, so I move plants to a bright window when spikes start to grow. Even without flowers the thin leaves are attractive. *V.splendens* and its hybrids are spectacular for dark-green leaves barred maroon-brown. The flower spike is orange to red with small yellow flowers appearing between the bracts. Color will last at least two months. After the rosette blooms it will form small plants in the center, then die. Pot vrieseas as suggested for guzmanias, keep roots lightly moist, fill cups with water every few days.

19
Propagation — Increasing Beauty Under Lights

Propagating houseplants under lights is a joy because success is the rule rather than the exception. Controlled temperatures and bright but not hot light give seeds a sturdy start. Cuttings root quickly and sometimes even flower in the propagation flat. You will be dealing with two basic types of propagation with your houseplants, vegetative or asexual and sexual.

Asexual

To grow new plants that exactly duplicate the parent in all respects (genetically), propagate asexually from vegetative sections. These include stems, tip cuttings, bulblets, runners, clump divisions, leaf cuttings, and offsets. Actual pieces of a "parent" plant produce duplicates unless cells are changed by a rare mutation, something that is uncommon but does occasionally occur, especially with African-violet hybrids. Advanced vegetative propagation, used with orchids, begonias, and many commercial crops, involves the culturing of cells on nutrient agar. This method, called meristem propagation, quickly provides thousands of plants identical to the superior donor.

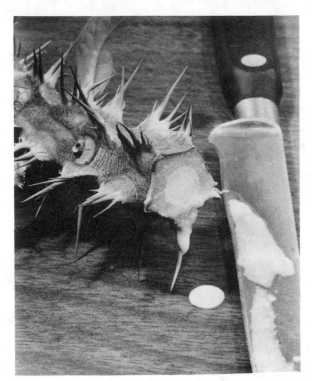

Euphorbia Keysii bleeds milky sap when cut for propagation, a characteristic of the genus.

After four months this tip cutting has established itself and begins to branch out (left), while the formerly leggy plant at right produces side branches after having the top removed. *Euphorbia Keysii* is an everblooming hybrid crown-of-thorns, excellent under lights.

Leaf cuttings, some with new plantlets. *Sansevieria hanii* (bottom), *Peperomia obtusifolia* (top right), *P.sandersii*.

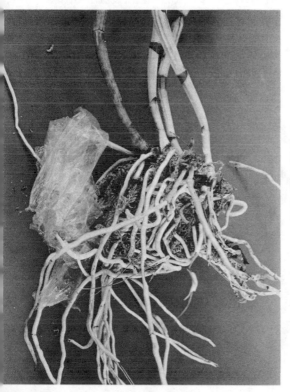

Cattleya-type orchids can be divided for additional plants, like this clump of pseudobulbs which was rooted in unmilled sphagnum before being cut from the main plant. New lead is at top left.

Sexual Reproduction

Seeds increase plants sexually by producing offspring that carry characteristics of the male and female gametes (reproductive cells). Usually two different plants are cross-pollinated to reproduce seedlings that mature to plants showing features of both pod (female) and pollen (male) parents. However most houseplants will accept pollen from their own flowers and form seed in what is called a self-cross. In this case, the resulting plants are more likely to be similar to the parent, but they will not be as uniform as in asexual propagation.

Creating hybrids involves sexual reproduction in a search for the ideal combination of characteristics from each parent. For example, you might have a pure-white gloxinia (*Sinningia* hybrid) that grows tall but want a pink bloom on a plant of moderate size. By crossing the tall white gloxinia with a dwarf red gloxinia, you might obtain some compact, pink-flowered hybrids. In any case, the offspring will genetically combine characteristics of both parents.

Sexual reproduction of orchids involves sowing minute seeds on nutrient agar in sterile flasks. These seedlings are ready for transplanting.

6 Years   5   4   3   2   1   6 mo.

Stages in growth for cattleya-type orchids show normal flowering in six years, but this time may be somewhat shortened with long-day culture under lights. (Rod McLellan Co. photo)

Special Seed

Commercial seedmen often offer seed of carefully controlled hybrids and thus are able to predict what the resulting plants will look like. Hybrids from seed you obtain by crossing different plants in your collection are usually less predictable but more exciting for being your own creations. Another source of unusual houseplant seed are the seed funds of tropical plant societies (see Chapter 21).

Rieger begonia 'Aphrodite Rose' is renewed as a stem cutting in a mix of perlite and milled sphagnum moss, now ready for potting.

233

Standard Gro-Lux are my favorite for starting seed but my tests with the newer Agro-Lite show that they are also excellent for starting seed or making vegetative propagations. Cool-White and Warm-White lamps work well for propagation, especially if plants also receive some sunlight, but the horticultural lamps are the most efficient for both seed-growing and asexual propagation. You can use the same lamps for propagation as have given you good results with mature plants indoors.

Temperature

With warm 75° nights vegetative propagations root faster, but you can also get satisfactory if somewhat slower rooting with nights in the 60's. Seeds need more precise temperatures

Air-layering this leggy *Dieffenbachia picta* cultivar begins by slicing halfway through the stem, dusting the cut with Rootone powder, then squeezing the ball of moist unmilled sphagnum moss around the cut, and covering with clear plastic, held at both ends with plastic Polytwist or a similar plant tie.

for optimum germination. Consult the seed envelopes for the germinating range best suited to each species. Seed offered in plant-society magazines is usually described with notes on how to grow the plants, including the best temperature range. You will find a useful centerfold of seed-growing temperatures and germination times in the catalogue of Geo. W. Park Seed Co. (See Chapter 21 list.)

A useful general range for germinating tropical seeds in 75°-80°. Bottom heat from a soil cable or from light fixtures under the seed flats will encourage even germination. Once seedlings have fully expanded their leaves, begin to gradually lower temperatures until nights are in the low 70's; this will result in more compact growth.

Procedures

Root vegetative propagations in moist, medium-grade perlite or a one-to-one mix of perlite with milled sphagnum moss. Only if you must have a mix that holds a lot of water for

After several weeks new roots will be seen through the clear plastic; the rooted top is ready to be cleanly cut just below the roots and potted alone. Save the base since it will usually sprout new shoots.

Favorite rex begonias can be increased by rooting healthy middle-aged leaves on a sphagnum-perlite mix. This clump of plantlets grew from a single 'Shirt Sleeves' leaf.

several days would I recommend vermiculite for vegetative propagation. Many tip cuttings and some leaves will root in plain water although plantlets will be stronger if you use a quarter-strength chemical houseplant fertilizer. Pot plantlets before roots grow beyond 2 inches.

Damp-Off Protection

A fungus problem that often kills seedlings or rooted cuttings is called damp-off. Associated rots can cause loss of valuable propagations, but you can protect plants with a drench of Benlate (Benomyl), a systemic fungicide, and Dexon, a chemical that checks root rots. Soak the propagating mix with this solution the day before you sow seeds or set in cuttings. The solution may also be poured on plants if trouble occurs after planting.

Seed Sowing

Sow seed on the surface of moist milled sphagnum moss, a mixture of perlite one-to-one with milled sphagnum moss (my favorite), or on a commercially prepared seed-sowing mix, such as Park's Sure-Fire Sowing mix. Fine seeds, like those of begonias, gesneriads, etc., should be misted with warm water, but don't cover them with any planting mix.

Larger seed, like those of amaryllis, geraniums, and many herbs, should be lightly covered with a one-quarter to one-half inch of the sowing mix, then gently watered in. Place seed flats 4 to 6 inches under lamps for even germination and sturdy seedlings. Miniature plastic greenhouses, seed-sowing trays with clear plastic covers, and terrarium-type containers will provide high humidity around young plants, but this extra

Practical helps for growing seeds under lights include a plastic compartment flat, at top left; Jiffy pots which are flat when dry (bottom left) but swell when watered before planting. The miniature plastic greenhouse at top right is ideal for sowing small seed on top of a perlite-milled sphagnum moss mixture.

protection is not required if relative humidity in your light garden is 60 to 70 percent. If you do use covered containers, be sure to provide some air circulation once seed germinates.

Ferns

Ferns reproduce from spores that form in groups called sori underneath the fronds. You can grow more ferns by collecting spores and sowing them on moist milled sphagnum or the one-to-one mix with perlite. Before new fronds appear, the spores grow into a green mosslike form. When water washes over this beginning stage (prothallium growth), an exchange of male and female cells takes place. Once this fertilization occurs, the young ferns will begin to sprout fronds.

Spores of a pteris species I sowed on the perlite-sphagnum moss mixture showed green prothalliums in four weeks under Wide-Spectrum Gro-Lux lamps. Once this green misty growth appears, it is important to spray the surface with warm water as an aid to fertilization. Some species may take several months before any green is seen. Most will begin growing fronds within a year. There is nothing wrong with mixing spores from several species. An interesting hybrid may result when two kinds of spores cross-fertilize.

Divide mature clumps of ferns into smaller sections if you wish to increase them. Davallias, *Polypodium aureum,* and other species with thick creeping rhizomes can grow from rhizome sections. Cultivars of the Boston fern (*Nephrolepsis exaltata*) send out threadlike rhizomes that root and sprout new plants if weighted down on moist sphagnum with a crock.

20
If Pests or Disease Strike

Your houseplants will seldom suffer from pests or disease if you use only pasteurized potting soil, maintain good air circulation, and isolate new arrivals until you are certain they harbor no harmful organisms. Normal biological occurrences, such as yellowing of lower foliage, frighten some people into thinking the worst. However most foliage troubles are due either to the *normal* falling of older leaves or improper environmental conditions, rather than pests or disease.

Root Health

Healthy roots are necessary for attractive foliage and flowers. Overwatering, extreme binding of roots due to being in the same pot too long, and extreme drying can all kill roots. With injured roots a plant begins to cut down on above-ground demands, mainly by slowing top growth and losing leaves.

Foliage Facts

Low humidity, for all indoor plants except cactus, causes leaves to curl or drop. If conditions are both dry and hot the leaves may get brown edges. Soaking the roots does not completely compensate for lack of moisture in the air. Therefore strive to maintain a minimum of 40 to 50 percent humidity where you wish to have healthy plants.

Cold water or too strong fertilizer will cause leaves to develop brown spots. Any water that touches leaves, especially the fuzzy foliage of gesneriads, should be room temperature. Fertilizers are safe in solution but only when mixed according to directions or weaker. Some insecticides may also cause foliage damage but without causing permanent harm.

Shower Time

Most houseplants will make healthier growth if you provide artificial rain in the form of an occasional warm gentle shower. Place the largest plants in the bathroom tub or shower stall, then wash off the leaves with a gentle lukewarm spray. One of the flexible hand showers or shampoo hoses is an excellent device for this gentle task.

Smaller plants growing together can be washed easily where they grow, but take care not to wet any electrical connections. To avoid problems with fungus and rot from wet foliage, do the showering at the start of the light period. This would be in the morning for plants that also receive daylight. After the washing, be sure that air circulation in the growing area is good so that foliage will dry before late afternoon.

Precautions

Species with fuzzy leaves sometimes develop spots if the water is too cold or too warm. If you are careful not to wet leaves except with room-temperature water, you can avoid spotting. Leaves may also be cleaned by blowing off dirt with a rubber syringe. The best kind is sold as a solder-blower by the Brookstone Company (see Chapter 21).

Some people use a soft brush to clean foliage on gesneriads. This is an excellent tool but be sure to wash it between plants unless you are positive that all the plants are pestfree; the brush is a perfect way to transfer pests or fungus spores from specimen to specimen.

Treatment for Pests

Wash off any pests you find. Use lukewarm water in a fairly strong stream to dislodge them and wash them down the drain. Then for complete protection, spray with an insecticide. Relatively safe are Black Leaf-40 (nicotine sulfate), which needs to be mixed with a warm soapy solution as from Ivory Flakes. Natural plant compounds, such as pyrethrum, are similar to nicotine sulfate in effectiveness as a contact poison, but none does as complete a job of killing pests as the modern chemicals.

Follow directions carefully. Too much insecticide will harm plants; too little will permit pests to build up a resistance. The insecticides listed below are safe for most houseplants, but

Insecticides can cause temporary damage to flowers and immature foliage.

always read label information for special cautions. For example, malathion is effective against many pests but it will burn or kill kalanchoes and some other succulents.

Add several drops of fish emulsion per gallon of spray solution to help the chemical stick on foliage. If you choose to use aerosal sprays, be sure to hold the can two to three feet away and let only the mist fall on the leaves. Apply insecticides and fungicides when temperatures are between 70 and 80°. Some sprays will cause foliage injury if applied when temperatures are above 85°.

Avoid getting spray on the lamps unless you plan to clean the glass later with a damp cloth. Accumulations of spray cut down light output. One spraying usually does not kill all pests since eggs may hatch later so eight to ten days after the first application, use the spray again. If a heavy infestation of pests or bad fungus attack occurs, isolate the affected plants until they are clean again. These are the most common houseplant pests:

Aphids: Sucking insects that cluster on new shoots and flower buds where they reproduce at a startling rate. Aphids may be brown or green and can be seen without a magnifying glass. Isotox or a similar complete spray will kill them.

Cyclamen mite: A nearly microscopic pest, very hard to see even with a magnifying glass, but twisted growth and distorted flowers will occur when cyclamen mites infest plants. African-violets and other gesneriads are most susceptible. Since these mites dig into tissues at the crown or growing point they are difficult to kill. The best "treatment" is to throw away infested plants. Next best is to isolate them and soak with a Kelthane spray. Repeat in eight days and again for a third treatment in eight days.

Mealybugs: These are cotton-like sucking pests that cluster in new growth and between stems and leaves.

Remove all you can by washing with soapy water, then drench with Isotox or malathion. Use Black Leaf-40 on ferns and succulents.

Red Spider Mites: These red-green mites first attack the undersides of foliage. Heavy infestations turn leaves yellow; fine webs will be seen. Light infestations are best identified with a magnifying glass, which will reveal the tiny moving mites on the undersurfaces of leaves. These pests thrive in dry places so misting leaves underneath will discourage but not kill them. Spray with Kelthane, especially the reverse of foliage. If the mites return after 8-10 days, spray again but with malathion.

Scale: Scales look like small lumps of sap or wax on stems or leaf veins. Some species are white, others dark brown, but all are dangerous for plants because they suck away nutrients. Scrub off all the scales you can find; an old toothbrush and soapy water will do the job. Then spray with Isotox or a similar all-purpose spray.

Slugs and snails ruin buds and tender stems.

243

Slugs and Snails: Remove any pests you find because they will eat leaves, buds, stems. Maintain a clean collection so snails and slugs will have no place to hide. Spread slug pellets or drench with a metaldehyde solution like Slugit.

Springtails: These infest the soil around plants that are kept moist. Drench the soil with a 57 percent malathion solution, one teaspoon malathion to one gallon of warm water, or lightly dust malathion powder over the soil surface.

Whiteflies: Tiny sucking insects, some with white wings. Spray with Isotox. Repeat in eight to ten days, cover especially undersides of foliage.

Combination Treatments

The systemic fungicide Benlate (Benomyl) is compatible with most insecticides and can thus be applied in the same spray. Recent studies indicate Benlate helps control red spider mites. When I spray with Malathion or Kelthane I always add Benlate to the solution. This controls fungus, helps stop spider mites, and adds to the effectiveness of the insecticide.

The solid yellow Vapona-impregnated strips, such as the Shell No-Pest strips, are useful in discouraging insect infestations. The Vapona strips are safe to hang in a basement, porch, or greenhouse light-garden area but they should not be used in living rooms, bedrooms, kitchens, or other places where people live or food is prepared. Read directions on the package regarding the number of strips to use per room.

Iron

Citrus trees, gardenias, hibiscus, and other indoor tropicals may develop yellow foliage when they do not have enough

Sap-sucking white flies and aphid-like young attack the undersides of *Melaleuca hypericifolia* leaves.

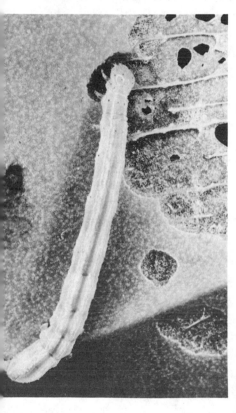

Caterpillars may hatch from eggs layed on foliage while houseplants are outdoors for the summer. Remove the pests and spray with a contact insecticide if many are present.

Powdery mildew attacks a *Begonia* 'Schwabenland' leaf.

iron. Other mineral deficiencies can also cause this yellowing or chlorosis but lack of iron is the most common. Treat the foliage with a spray of Green Garde or a similar water-soluble iron. A sprinkle of Green Garde powder on the soil will furnish iron over a period of months.

Diseases

In a healthy environment, disease is seldom a problem but from time to time a fungus may attack weak plants or rot cause a too-moist plant to die back. Modern fungicides are effective against many harmful organisms, but the ultimate cure is adequate spacing of plants, moving air, and dry foliage at night.

Fungus

Powdery mildew and black spot on miniature roses, Rieger begonias, and other susceptible species can be controlled with Benomyl fungicide (Benlate by DuPont), a systemic fungicide powder designed to be mixed with water and applied to all parts of a plant. The fungicide is absorbed systemically and thus kills fungus from within the plant.

Sulfur spray or dust, such as Ortho Flotox, is effective against mildew. Karathane fungicide, mixed at one-half teaspoon per gallon of water, is another excellent preventer of mildew. Karathane can be combined with most insecticides but should not be used in combination with sulfur.

Always cut away infected portions of a plant and discard them where no spores can reach healthy plants. Root rots may occur with overwatering or because a plant is weak and spores happen to get a hold. Drench the soil and the lower parts of the plant with a solution of Dexon—one teaspoon per gallon of water. Cut away rotted parts into sound tissue, keep cuts dry until they heal, increase air circulation.

Botrytis may cause seedlings to die at the soil line, or cause plant stems to get soft and rot away. The cure is to spray with Captan or Daconil, increase spacing, improve air circulation, keep foliage dry. If you do not know what pest or disease is troubling your plants, get advice from your county agent, a local botanical garden, or university.

Algae

Although algae is really not a disease it can cause gravel or perlite in light-garden trays to turn green and thus cut down on light for the plants. An excellent control for algae that is also safe for plants is Physan (formally called Consan). This is a clear liquid that is mixed at one teaspoon per gallon of water to spray on seedlings or over pot tops to prevent growth of algae and some forms of fungus. At a stronger dilution, one tablespoon per gallon, it will sanitize pots and trays. The weaker dilution of one teaspoon per gallon is recommended for algae control if it is applied monthly. Physan is offered by several orchid nurseries.

21

Plant Societies and Sources of Equipment

Your appreciation of ornamental plants, and continued success in growing them to perfection will be greatly increased by membership in the horticultural societies. As a member you receive helpful illustrated publications, are put in touch with gardeners of similar interests, have access to unusual seeds, and in many cases will be invited to join a local chapter.

The plant societies listed here are nonprofit organizations devoted to educational activities and research. Some of them do not have a regular office staff or address, so from time to time an address may change with the election of a new secretary. However by writing to the address listed here, you will be put in touch with the new officer to obtain membership details.

Most of the groups have reasonable dues $5.00 to $15.00 a year, a bargain considering the usefulness of many society publications. Your local library, garden club, or botanical garden may have sample publications from the societies, all worth seeing before you choose which groups to join.

Publications of tropical plant societies inform readers of the latest ornamental plants available and detail modern methods of culture.

Indoor Plant Societies

The African Violet Society of America
P.O. Box 1326
Knoxville, Tenn. 37901

Monthly *African Violet* magazine with color.

The American Begonia Society
6333 West 84th Place
Los Angeles, Calif. 90045

Monthly *Begonian* magazine, seed fund, local chapters.

The American Gloxinia and Gesneriad
  Society
P.O. Box 174
New Milford, Conn. 06776

Bimonthly *Gloxinian* magazine, seed fund, local chapters.

The American Horticultural Society
Mount Vernon, Virginia 22121

National society for the advancement of ornamental horticulture. Quarterly *American Horticulturist*, with color.

The American Ivy Society
c/o Horticultural Society of New York
128 West 58th St.
New York, N.Y. 10019

Relatively new group devoted to the study and culture of ivies.

The American Orchid Society
Botanical Museum of Harvard University
Cambridge, Mass. 02138

Monthly magazine with color
A.O.S. *Bulletin*, local chapters.

The American Plant Life Society
Box 150
La Jolla, Calif. 92037

Devoted to amaryllis and related
genera. Yearly *Plant Life* book
included with membership fee.

The Bromeliad Society
P.O. Box 3279
Santa Monica, Calif. 90403

Bimonthly color-illustrated *Journal*,
local chapters.

Cactus and Succulent Society of America
Box 167
Reseda, Calif. 91335

Bimonthly magazine covers succulents on an international level.

Indoor Light Gardening Society of
America
128 West 58th St.
New York, N.Y. 10019

Bimonthly magazine, seed fund,
local chapters.

The International Geranium Society
c/o Arthur Thiede
11960 Pascal Ave.
Colton, Calif. 92324

Quarterly *Journal*.

Gesneriad Society International
P.O. Box 549
Knoxville, Tenn. 37901

Bimonthly *Gesneriad-Saintpaulia
News* shared with Saintpaulia
International, in color.

Los Angeles International Fern Society
2423 Burritt Ave.
Redondo Beach, Calif. 90278

Monthly bulletin, fern-spore exchange.

The Orchid Digest Corp.
c/o Mrs. Forest W. Slack, Sec.
25 Ash Ave.
Corte Madera, Calif. 94925

Bimonthly color-illustrated *Orchid
Digest*.

Saintpaulia International Society
P.O. Box 549
Knoxville, Tenn. 37901

Shares color-illustrated *GSN
Magazine* with the American
Gesneriad Society.

Plants and Growing Supplies

You may find choice houseplants and useful growing supplies at local garden centers. In fact, a specialist grower who features unusual tropical plants may live nearby. However you will seldom find all of the plants or supplies you want locally. Therefore I present this extensive listing of sources for unusual plants and the supplies required to grow them under lights. Some catalogues are free, others cost a small amount. The plant publications are worth having for illustrations, descriptions, and culture hints slanted to those specimens offered in each catalog.

Specialists' catalogues will be the first to list exciting new cultivars, so the best way to keep up to date with what is being offered is to obtain the plant catalogues. If you are ordering any of the plants I mention in this book be sure to use the

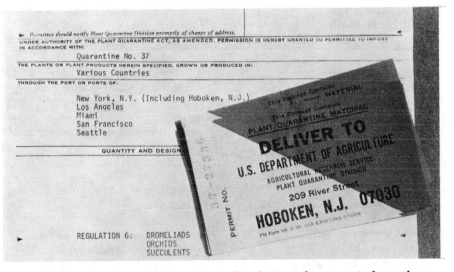

To bring back plants from your travels, obtain a free permit from the United States Department of Agriculture Plant Quarantine Division. Request the booklet giving import rules when you write for the permit. Collect only sample species and observe all local conservation laws.

scientific name. Popular or common names may be fun but since they vary from region to region, you may not obtain the desired plant unless you use the internationally accepted scientific label.

SOURCE

OFFERINGS

Abbey Garden
176 Toro Canyon Road
Carpinteria, Ca. 93013

Comprehensive illustrated
catalogue of succulents, 25 cents.

Aladdin Industries Inc.
P.O. Box 10666
Nashville, Tenn. 37210

Creators of the Phyto-Gro
Chamber. Free leaflet.

Alberts & Merkel Bros.
P.O. Box 537
Boynton Beach, Fla. 33435

Rare tropicals including bromeliads
and orchids. Catalogue 50¢.

American Louver Co.
7700 Austin Ave.
Skokie, Ill. 60076

Manufacturers of Paracube louvers
and similar wedged panels for
shielding lamps. Free bulletins on
louver styles, *no retail sales.*

Ames Greenhouses Inc.
Route 2, East 13th St.
Ames, Iowa 50010

Cyclone Impatiens hybrids derived
from New Guinea species. Free list.

Armstrong Associates Inc.
P.O. Box 94
Kennebunk, Maine 04043

Insectivorous species. Catalogue 25
cents.

Arthur Eames Allgrove
North Wilmington, Mass. 01887

Terrarium plants, supplies. Catalogue
50 cents.

ASG Industries Inc.
P.O. Box 929
Kingsport, Tenn. 37662

Manufacturers of water-white
crystal glass panels, some with
prismatic surfaces. Free folder on
types, but no retail sales; see
samples at local dealers.

Beahm Gardens
2686 Paloma St.
Pasadena, Calif. 91107

Epiphyllums, Rhipsalis and Hoyas.
Send large stamped envelope or
first-class postage for list.

SOURCE	OFFERINGS
The Beall Co. Vashon Island, Washington 98070	Orchids, especially unusual hybrids of *Oncidium* and *Odontoglossum*. Free list.
Brookstone Co. Peterborough, N.H. 03458	Free catalogue lists some unusual gardening tools.
John Brudy's Rare Plant House P.O. Box 1348 Cocoa Beach, Fla. 32931	$1.00 color catalog of tropical plant seeds.
Buell's Greenhouses Eastford, Conn. 06242	African-violets and other gesneriads. Free list for large stamped envelope.
W. Atlee Burpee Co. Box 6929 Philadelphia, Pa. 19132	Free catalogue includes some light fixtures and houseplants.
Carobil Farm and Greenhouses Church Road, Rd.1 Brunswick, Ma. 04011	Free list of unusual geraniums and fuchsias.
Carter and Holmes Orchids P.O. Box 491 Newberry, S. Carolina 29108	Orchids, including mericlones, plus ferns and other houseplants. Free catalogue.
L. Easterbrook Greenhouses 10 Craig Street Butler, Ohio 44822	Tropical houseplants, many terrarium species. Catalog $1.00
Edelweiss Gardens 54 Robbinsville-Allentown Rd. Robbinsville, N.J. 08691	35 cents list includes many unusual houseplants. Visitors welcome at nursery.
Encap Products Co. P.O. Box 278 Mt. Prospect, Ill. 60056	Green Garde iron and insecticides.
Environment One Corp. 2773 Balltown Rd. Schenectady, N.Y. 12309	Manufacturer of Phytarium growth chamber. Free booklet.
Fischer Greenhouses Linwood, N.J. 08221	Catalogue 20 cents—mainly African-violets and other gesneriads.

SOURCE	OFFERINGS
Fleco Industries 3347 Halifax St. Dallas, Texas 75247	Free catalogue of light stands.
Floralite Co. 4124 East Oakwood Rd. Oak Creek, Wis. 53154	Fluorescent light fixtures, water sprayers, stands. Free list.
Arthur Freed Orchids Inc. 5731 South Bonsall Drive Malibu, Calif. 90265	Phalaenopsis and their hybrids. Many dwarf growers, unusual ascocendas. Free color catalogue.
The Green House 9515 Flower St. Bellflower, Calif. 90706	Gro-Cart plant stands. Free leaflet.
GTE Sylvania Lighting Center Danvers, Mass. 01923	Engineering bulletins related to Gro-Lux and Wide-Spectrum Gro-Lux in horticulture.
House Plant Corner P.O. Box 810 Oxford, Md. 21654	Catalogue 20 cents lists very complete assortment of growing supplies, light stands.
H. L. Hubbell Inc. P.O. Box 107 Dept. CF-1 Zeeland, Michigan 49464	Original funiture incorporating fluorescent fixtures. Free folder.
Hyponex Co. Copley, Ohio 44321	Chemical fertilizers and growing aids. Free catalogue.
Margaret Ilgenfritz Orchids Monroe, Mich. 48161	Specialist in species. $2.00 color catalogue has many compact types.
P. de Jager & Sons. South Hamilton, Mass. 01982 *or* 132 Dinnick Crescent Toronto, Canada	Quality bulbs including some hardy miniature species of crocus, cyclamen, and narcissus. Free color catalog.
Jensen Tool Co. 4117 North 44th St. Phoenix, Arizona 85018	Free catalog of unusual tools, many useful in light-gardening electrical work.
J & L Orchids 20 Sherwood Rd. Easton, Conn. 06612	Rare species orchids, especially small growing masdevallias and others suited to light gardens.

SOURCE	OFFERINGS
Johnson Cactus Gardens 2735 Olive Hill Rd. Fallbrook, Calif. 92028	Well-illustrated catalogue of cactus and other succulents, 25 cents.
Jones & Scully Inc. 2200 North West 33rd Ave. Miami, Fla. 33142	Orchid specialists. Special listing of orchids suitable under lights. $3.00 color catalogue.
Kartuz Greenhouses Wilmington, Mass. 01887	Miniature to dwarf gesneriads and begonias. Catalogue 50 cents. Many unusuals suitable to light gardens.
Lauray of Salisbury Undermountain Rd. Salisbury, Conn. 06068	Gesneriads, begonias, succulents. Catalogue 50 cents.
Lehua Anthurium Nursery 80 Kokea St. Hilo, Hawaii 96720	Free listing of anthuriums includes some unique dwarf cultivars, perfect under lights.
Robert Lester Orchids 280 West 4th St. New York, N.Y. 10014	Unusual species including night-fragrant Africans. Supplies and light equipment.
Logee's Greenhouses Danielson, Conn 06239	Wide assortment of tropicals listed in color illustrated $1.00 catalogue. Visitors welcome.
Lord & Burnham Co. Irvington, N.Y. 10533	Free folder of greenhouses, an indoor garden case, supplies.
Lyndon Lyon Dolgeville, N.Y. 13329	Free listing of unique new African violets. Send stamp.
Marko 94 Porete Ave. North Arlington, N.J. 07032	Fixtures with wedged louvers to hide lamps, also styrene grates. Free list.
Rod McLellan Co. 1450 El Camino Real South San Francisco, Calif. 94080	$1.00 color catalogue shows wide selection of unusual orchids including new meristems. Visitors welcome.
Mellinger's 2310 West South Range Rd. North Lima, Ohio 44452	Comprehensive catalogue of plants and supplies is free.

SOURCE	OFFERINGS
Merry Gardens Camden, Maine 04843	Catalogue 50 cents, illustrated booklet $1.00. Unusual tropicals in many genera.
Moore Miniature Roses 2519 East Nobile Ave. Visalia, Calif. 93277	Free color folder shows new miniature roses.
Nor'East Miniature Roses Box 852 Gloucester, Ma. 01930	Free catalogue of excellent new miniature roses with many that thrive under lights.
George W. Park Seed Co. Greenwood, South Carolina 29646	Free catalogue of seeds, supplies, light stands, tubes, timers, culture notes.
Robert B. Peters Co. 2833 Pennsylvania St. Allentown, Pa. 18104	Free list of chemical fertilizers.
Plantation Garden Products P.O. Box 127 Boynton Beach, Fla. 33435	20 cent catalogue lists supplies for orchids and bromeliads.
R. J. Rands Orchids 15322 Mulholland Drive Los Angeles, Calif. 90024	Unusual Paphiopedilum hybrids, many warm-growing hybrids with attractive mottled leaves. Free list.
Rohm and Haas Co. P.O. Box 9730, Dept. JC Philadelphia, Pa. 19140	Booklets and directions for working with Plexiglas acrylic sheets, 50 cents.
Rosco Laboratories, Inc. 36 Bush Ave. Port Chester, N.Y. 10573	Unique Roscoflex reflection media in rolls 48" x 30 ft. includes tough wear-resistant mirror and pebble surfaces. Sample book of reflection materials—$1.50.
Santa Barbara Orchid Estates 1250 Orchid Drive Santa Barbara, Calif. 93111	Free listing of cymbidiums and Yamamoto dendrobium hybrids.
John Scheepers Inc. 63 Wall St. New York, N.Y. 10005	Free flower bulb catalogue lists some hardy miniatures, plus lily of the valley pips.

SOURCE	OFFERINGS
Seaborn Del Dios Nursery Box 455 Escondido, Calif. 92025	Bromeliads, cycads, and palms.
Shaffer's Tropical Gardens 1220 41st Ave. Santa Cruz, Calif. 95060	Phalaenopsis specialists. Free color catalogue.
Shoplite Co. 566 Franklin Ave. Nutley, N.J. 07110	Complete 25 cent catalogue lists wide selection of fixtures, stands, tubes, parts.
SOS Photo-Cine Optics Inc. 315 West 43rd St. New York, N.Y. 10036	Theatrical light fixtures, lamps, colored gels. Roscolene and Gelatran.
Southern Gardens P.O. Box 547 Riverview, Fla. 33569	Free list of unusual succulents and some supplies.
Fred A. Stewart Co. 1212 East Las Tunas Drive San Gabriel, Calif. 91778	Orchids, especially cattleya hybrids including new dwarfs perfect under lights. $1.00 color illustrated catalogue.
Terrestris 409 East 60th St. New York, N.Y. 10022	Indoor plants. Catalogue 50 cents.
Texas Greenhouse Co. 2717 St. Louis Ave. Ft. Worth, Texas 76110	Free catalogue of growing supplies, including fans, watering devices, humidifiers.
Thompson & Morgan Inc. P.O. Box 24 Somderdale, N.J. 08083	Free catalog includes some seed of unusual indoor plants.
Tinari Greenhouses 2325 Valley Rd. Huntington Valley, Pa. 19006	Light fixtures, African violets and other gesneriads. Catalogue 20 cents.
Tube Craft Inc. 1311 West 80th St. Cleveland, Ohio 44102	Free folder shows unique Flora Carts and related light garden supplies.

Velco Importers
3171 Purdue Ave.
Los Angeles, Calif. 90066

Extensive offering of bromeliads.
Free catalogue.

Verilux Inc.
35 Mason St.
Greenwich, Conn. 06830

Verilux TruBloom lamps, free
folder.

West Coast Gesneriads
2179 44th Ave.
San Francisco, Calif. 94116

Unusual gesneriads listed in 10 cent
catalogue.

Whistling Hill
Box 27
Hamburg, N.Y. 14075

Rare gesneriads. List 25 cents.

Wilson Brothers
Roachdale, Indiana 46172

Free catalogue lists mainly
geraniums of all kinds, some
supplies, other plants.

Rudolf Ziesenhenne
1130 North Milpas St.
Santa Barbara, Calif. 93103

Specialist in unusual begonias,
seeds, and plants.

The Old Farmer's Almanac
Yankee Inc.
Dublin, N.H. 03444

Old Farmer's Almanac has day-
length charts. Available by mail for
$1.00 postpaid or 75 cents at news-
stands.

Bibliography

Cloudsley Thompson, J. L. *The Zoology of Tropical Africa*. New York: W. W. Norton & Co., Inc., 1969.

Foster, Gordon F. *Ferns to Know and Grow*. New York: Hawthorn Books, Inc., 1971.

Graf, Alfred B. *Exotic Plant Manual*. New Jersey: Julius Roehrs Co., 1970.

The Illuminating Engineering Society. *Lighting Design and Application* New York. Monthly journal.

Lamb, Edgar and Brian. *Encyclopedia of Cacti*. New York: Macmillan Co., Inc., 1970.

McDonald, Elvin. *Little Plants for Small Spaces*. New York: Popular Library, 1974.

Wilson, Helen Van Pelt. *The African-Violet Book*. New York: Hawthorn Books, Inc., 1970.

——. *The Joy of Geraniums*. New York: William Morrow and Co., Inc., 1972.

Withner, Carl, editor. *The Orchids, A Scientific Survey*. New York: The Ronald Press Co., 1959.

——. *The Orchids, Scientific Studies*. New York: John Wiley and Sons, 1974.

Index

Acchmea, 224–225
  chantinii, 224
  fasciata, 224
  miniata var. *discolor*, 225
Achimens, 115, 117
  'Crimson Beauty', 117
  'Tarantella', 117
  'Menuett', 118
Acid-alkaline balance, 110
  testing for, 110
Adaptability of houseplants, 13–14
Adiantum, 178
  hispidulum, 178
  tenerum 'Wrightii', 178
Adromischus, 198
  cooperi, 198
  festivus, 198
  maculatus, 198
Aerangis orchids, 137
  biloba, 137
  compta, 137
  rhodosticta, 137
Aeschynanthus, 114–115, 118, 122
  'Black Pagoda', 118
  lobbianus, 118
  micranthus, 118
  obconicus, 118
  parvifolius, 118
  pulcher, 118
  tricolor, 118
African blood-lilies, 219
African-Violet Book (Wilson), 123
African-violets, 7, 11, 35, 53, 71
  containers for, 87, 88
  fertilizers, 107, 108
  fixtures for, 21, 23, 53
  fluorescents and incandescents, 53–55, 117
  light and temperature, 77, 113–114
  light-hours and intensity, 36, 61, 113–114,
    116–117, 123
    watts per square foot, 36
  medium-light requirements, 61
  miniature, 122–123
  pests, 242
  potting mixes, 101

African-violets (*cont.*)
  propagating, 229
  temperatures for, 74, 77, 114
  watering, 94
Agapanthus 'Peter Pan', 209
Agave, 62, 196, 198
  filifera compacta, 198
  striata nana, 198
  victoriae-reginae, 198
Aglaonema, 61
  commutatum, 35
Agro-Lite (Westinghouse), 50
  for starting seeds, 234
Air circulation, 58, 83
  fresh air, 83
Air conditioning, effects of, 79
Air plants. *See* Bromeliads
Aladdin Industries, 25–26
Algae control, 247
Allard, H. A., 69–70
Allium schoenoprasum, 160
Allophyton mexicanum, 210
Alocasia, 166
  'Amazonica', 165
Aloe, 62, 193, 194–195
  bellatula, 198
  brevifolia depressa, 199
  haworthioides, 198–199
  humilis, 199
  jacunda, 198
  praetense, 198
  rauhii, 198
  variegata, 198
  vera, 199
Amaryllis, 73–74, 88, 218–219
  gracilis cultivars, 219
Amazon-lily, 219
American Horticulturist, 73
American Louver Company, 29
American Orchid Society, 128, 132
American Orchid Society Bulletin, 132
Amesiella philippinensis, 137
Ananas comosus
  variegatus, 225
  nanus, 225

Angelwings, 62, 180, 182
Angraecum orchids, 137
  magdalenae, 137
  philippinense, 137
Anoectochilus
  roxburghii, 152
  sikkimensis, 152
Anthurium, 61, 73, 107, 108, 166, 209
  andraeanum, 209
  bakeri, 166
  clarinevium, 166
  crystallinum, 166, 178
  polyschistum, 95
  scherzerianum, 209
    'Rothschildianum', 209
    'Album', 209
Aphelandra squarross, 70, 210
  'Dania', 210
Aphids, 242
Ascocentrum, 128, 137
  Ascocenda, 137
Ascofinetia, 145
  Nakamotoara (x *Ascocentrum* and *Vanda*),
    145
Asconopsis, 149
Asparagus densiflorus (syn A. *meyeri*), 178
Aspasia, 139
  principissa, 138–139
Aspidistra, 163
  elatior, 61
Aspoglossum, 146
Australian Orange blossom orchid, 151
Automatic timers, 6, 25, 27, 58, 75
Avocation of gardening, 7
Azalea, 108
  tree, 33

Bark chips, 100
Basement gardens, 7–8
Basil (*Ocimum basilicum*), 159
  'Dark Opal', 159
  minimum var., 159
Bay leaf (*Laurus nobilis*), 159–160
Beall Orchids, 131, 139–140, 146
Begonia, 11, 84, 122, 180–192
  acaulis, 182
  acida, 182, 185–186
  angelwing, 62, 180, 182, 185
  'Aries', 35
  aucalis, 186
  'Ballet', 185
  bowerae (eyelash begonia), 61, 182, 183, 186
    'China Doll', 186
    'Cleopatra', 182
    'Gaystar', 182, 183, 186
    'Maphil' ('Cleopatra'), 182
    nigramarga, 186

Begonia (*cont.*)
  'Brooks', 192
  cane-stem, 182
    angelwing hybrids, 185
  Christmas and winter-blooming, 70
  circline table lamp for, 23
  conchifolia, 186–187
  containers for, 86–87, 88
  cubensis, 182, 188
  eyelash. *See Begonia bowerae*
  fibrous-rooted, 183, 185–186
  foliosa, 188
  goegoensis, 182
  growth styles, 183–185
  hairy-leaved (hirsute), 185, 192
  lamps and light-hours, 35–36, 51, 180–182
    lamp watts per square foot, 36
    Wide Spectrum Gro-Lux for, 51
  leptotricha 'Wooly Bear', 192
  masoniana, 184
  'Muriel Gray', 186–187
  pests and disease, 190
  'Pinafore', 185
  potting mixes, 103
  'Priscilla Beck', 192
  prismatocarpa, 186
  propagation, 180, 229
  pustulata, 88, 186–187, 188
  rex hybrids, 61, 182–183, 186–188
    'It', 188
    'Merry Christmas', 187–188
    'Shirt Sleeves', 86, 188, 236
  rhizomatous selections, 182, 183, 186
  Rieger cultivars, 107, 189–190, 246
    'Aphrodite Pink', 189
    'Aphrodite Rose', 233
    'Bernsteins Gelbe', 189–190
    culture, 190
    elatior hybrids, 77, 183
    'Improved Schwabenland Orange', 181,
      189, 245
    light-hours and intensities, 191
    pruning plants, 191
    'Schwabenland Red', 190
    sources, 190
    watering and fertilizing, 190
  'San Miguel', 192
  schmidtiana, 182, 192
  semperflorens (wax) hybrids, 62, 180, 182
    183, 185
  'Shirt Sleeves', 86, 88, 236
  soil and fertilizer, 183
  solanthera, 173, 188
  strawberry-begonia, 172
  'Switzerland', 88
  'Tom Ment', 184, 185
  trailing, 188

Begonia (cont.)
  tuberous-rooted types, 70, 182–183, 188–189
    'Switzerland', 188–189
  venosa, 192
Beloperone guttata, 210
Benches and tables, for light gardens, 40
  wood preservative treatment, 40
Benlate (Benomyl), 236, 244, 246
Berkey Colortran Showlites, 30–31
Billbergia, 224–225
  nutans, 225
  zebrina, 225
Biophytum sensifivum, 166
Biorythms, 69
Black Leaf-40 (nicotine sulfate), 241, 242
Black Magic planter-mix, 116, 207
Black spot, 246
Blooming of plants
  effects of temperature, 74–75
  environmental factors, 69
  results under lights, 4
Boca hygroscopica, 118
Bookcase light gardens, 32–38, 54
  construction, 32, 34
  fixtures, 34–35
  foliage plants for, 163
  high-light, 36–37
  size and type of lamps, 35–36
Boston fern, 178
  cultivars, 238
Botrytis, 246
Bottle gardens, 10
Bougainvillea, 70, 210
Boxwood, miniature, 100
Brandywine 'Brilliant' orchid, 142
Brapasia Serene orchid, 138–139
Brassavola orchids, 139
  nodosa, 139
Brassia orchids, 139
  longissima x *gircoucliana*, 139
    Edvah Loo, 139
  maculata, 139
'Brazilian edelweiss', 126
Brewster Corporation, 41
Brightness, factor in growing plants under
    lights, 57
Broad-spectrum fluorescents, 50–51, 54
Bromeliads, 9, 11, 62, 73, 84, 222–228
  culture, 222–223
  epiphytic, 222–223
  light-hours and intensities, 223–224
    high-light requirements, 36, 51
  potting mixes, 99
  propagation, 224
  selections to grow, 224–228
  sunlight requirements, 15–16

Bulbs, 217–221
  after blooming, 217–218
  containers for, 88
  Dutch, 220
  flowering time, 221
  hardy, 220
  potting, 220–221
  rooting period, 221
  selection of, 220
Burns, treated with *aloe vera*, 199
Burrotail, 203
Buxus microphylla japonica, 166

Cacti, 193–208
  Christmas, 75, 206–208
  desert cacti, 204–206
  fertilizers, 196
  grafted 'Bunnies', 206
  high-light requirements, 36
  jungle, 194–195, 204, 206–208
    length-hours and intensities, 207
    propagation, 207
    soil for, 207
  light-hours and intensities, 14, 36, 194–196, 204
  orchid-cactus, 207
  pots for, 87, 196
  soils for, 106, 207
  summer growth, 196–197
  sunlight vs. fluorescents, 193–194
  Thanksgiving cactus, 206
Caladium, 111, 166
  'Candidium', 166
  humboldtii, 166
Calamondin orange (*Citrus mitis*), 211
Calathea, 167
  picturata 'Argentea', 167
Calla lilies, 220
Cape primrose (*Streptocarpus*), 114
Capsicum annuum conoides, 210–211
Captan spray, 246
Carissa grandiflora, 167
  nana compacta, 167
Carrion flower, 203
Cast-iron plant (*Aspidistra elatior*), 61
Catasetum orchids, 139–140
  pileatum, 139
  pileatum x *expansum*, 140
    Orchidglade, 140
  trulla x *fimbriatum*, 140
    Francis Nelson, 139–140
  warscewiczii, 139
Caterpillars, 245
Cathey, Dr. Henry M., 64–65
Cattleya hybrid orchids, 15, 62, 70, 128–129,
    131–132, 136, 140–142, 233
  aclandiae, 140

Cattleya hybrid orchids (cont.)
  aurantiaca, 140
  compact types, 140–142
    Le Chit Chat 'Tangerine', 141
  forbesii, 141
  intermedia, 141
    aquinii, 141
  trianaci, 135
  walkeriana, 141–142
    Brandywine 'Brilliant', 142
    hybrids with Sophronitis, 141–142
    Jewel Box 'Crimson Glory', 142
Cement or cinder-blocks, treated surfaces,
    40–41
Century plants (Agave), 62
Chamaeccereus silvestrii, 204
Chamaedorea elegans 'Bella', 167
Chinese evergreens (Aglaonema), 61
Chirita sinensis, 52, 119
Chives (Allium schoenoprasum), 160
Chlorophyll, 46–47
Chlorophytum comosum, 167
  variegatum, 167
  vittatum, 167, 168
Christmas cactus, 75, 206–208
Christmas-pepper, 210–211
Christmas poinsettia, 70, 200
Chrysanthemums, 70
Circline fixtures, 21, 23
Cissus (Grape-ivy), 61, 173
  antarica, 173
  discolor, 5
  rhombiafolia, 173
  striata, 173
Citris mitis, 211
Citrus shrubs, 108, 212
  iron deficiency, 244–246
Clay pots, unglazed, 85
  See also Containers
Climbers and creepers, 173–176
Codiaeum, 168
  'punctatum aureum', 168
  variegatum, 168
Coffea arabica, 168
Coleus, 71, 84
  blumei hybrids, 5, 35, 168
  salificolius, 165
Colmanara orchids, 146
Columnea, 119
  'Mary Ann', 119
  'Red Spur', 119
  trailing, 8
  'Yellow Hammer', 119
Combolite (Tube Craft Co.), 20
Comparettia macroplectron orchids, 142
Complete Book of Terrariums, The (Fitch),
    93

Containers, 85–93
  azalea pots, 85, 88
  bottom drainage material, 97
  choosing, 86–87
  display pots, 92
  fiberglass wicks, 90–91
  foamy plastic, 87
  Mexican animalito pots, 94
  moisture trays, 82, 97
  on wire grids or wood slats, 97
  orchids pots, 86
  plastic pots, 85
  self-watering, 89–90
  shallow pot or bulb pan, 85–86
  sizes and styles, 85–89
  square pots, 86
  terrariums, 92–93
  three-quarter-size azalea pots, 85–88
  undrained, 91–92
  watering methods, 93–98
Cool Beam bulb, 30
Cool-growing houseplants, 13
Cool Lux bulb, 30
Cool White tubes, 4–5, 10, 16, 48, 49, 51, 52,
    54
  brightness, 57
  for propagation, 234
Cornell University, 99
Crassula (jadeplant), 194–199
  argentea, 199
  coperi, 199
  lycopodioides, 199
  perforata, 199
  schmidtii, 199
Creepers and climbers, 5, 173–176
Crocus, 88, 220, 221
  autumn, 221
Crossandra infundibuliformis, 212
Crotons, 168
Crown-of-thorns, 200, 230
Crypthanthus, 226
  bivittatus, 226
  fosterianus, 226
  zonatus, 226
Cuprinol, wood preservative, 40
Cuttings for propagation, high-light
    requirements, 36–37
Cyanotis, 173
  kewensis, 173
  somaliensis, 173
Cyclamen mite, 242
Cycnoches (Swan orchids), 142
  ventricosum, 142
    chlorochilon, 142
    chlorochilon x mormodes colossus, 143
    'Ginger Shop', 143
    warscewiczii, 142

Cycocel for chemical dwarfing, 155–156
Cymbalaria muralis, 173
Cymbidium orchids, 133, 142
Cyperus alternifolius, 97

Daconil spray, 246
Damp-off protection, 236, 246
Davallia, 178, 238
  bullata mariesii, 178
  pentaphylla, 178
Day-length responses, 18, 58
  long-day plants, 70
  plant reactions to, 68–75
  research studies, 18
  short-day plants, 70
  variations in, 74
Daylight fluorescents, 16, 49, 54, 56
Day-neutral of intermediate cultivars, 70
Dendrobium orchids, 130, 142–143
  aggregatum, 143
  nobile, 143
  Yamamoto hybrids, 143
Desk or reading lamps, 6
Desktop oiroline fixtures, 21, 23
Devil's Ivy (*Pothos*), 61
Dexon fungicide, 98, 236, 246
Dieffenbachia, 168
  picta cultivar, 234
Diseases of houseplants, 246
  algae, 247
  fungus, 246–247
Distance and intensity of lamps, 38
Dizygotheca elegantissima, 169
Dolomite limestone powder, 100, 110
Doritaenopsis orchid, 149
Dracaena, 169
  godseffiana 'Florida Beauty', 169
  goldiena, 169
  sanderiana, 169
Dumbcanes, 168
Duro-Lite lamps, 29, 49
  Natur-Escent, 51
Dyckias, 222

Earth-stars, 226
Echeveria, 199
  derenbergii, 199
  elegans, 199
  pulvinata, 199
Echinocactus grusonii, 205
Edithcolea grandis, 199
Electric power
  conserving, 75
  energy-saving steps. 75
  grounding plugs and sockets, 39–40
  light gardens, 39
  power problems, 62–63
English ivy, 174

Environmental conditions, 58, 69, 76–84
Epicattleya hybrids, 144
Epidendrum orchids, 62, 128, 143–144
  anceps, 143
  ciliare, 143–144
  cochleatum, 144
Epiphyllum cultivars, 207–208
  'Elegantissimum', 208
Epiphytic orchids, 15–16, 96, 97, 99, 132–134
Episcia (orchids), 14, 16, 74, 115, 119–120
  cupreata, 120
    'Acajou', 120
    'Cygnet', 119–120
Espostoa lanata, 206
Eucharis grandiflora, 219
Euconis, 219
  bicolor, 219
Euphorbia, 62, 194, 200
  'Bojeri', 200
  cristata, 200
  Keysii, 200, 230
  lactea, 200
  pulcherrima (Christmas poinsettia), 70, 200
  splendens, 200
Evergreens, 13
  Chinese, 61
Exacum affine (Persian-violet), 70, 212
  'Midget' hybrids, 49, 212
Exotic plants under lights, 8

Farmer's Almanac, 74
Faucaria, 200
  tigrina, 200
  tuberculosa, 200
Ferns, 7, 13, 15, 54, 84, 163–164, 176–179
  Boston ferns, 178, 238
  dwarf holly ferns, 179
  low-light requirements, 6, 61, 176
  maidenhair, 178
  pests, 242
  propagating, 238
  rabbit's foot ferns, 178
  staghorn or elkhorn, 179
Fertilizers, 103–110
  acid-alkaline balance, 110
  compressed, 108–110
  constant weak application, 106
  fish emulsion formulas, 105
  foliage plants, 164
  formulas, 108
  nutrients (nitrogen, phosphorus and
      potassium), 105
    trace elements, 104
  for orchids, 134
  seaweed, 106
  slow-release products, 97, 107, 134

Fertilizers (*cont.*)
  water-soluble, 105
Ficus, ornamental figs, 61
  creeping, 6
  diversifolia, 169
  pumilia
    minima, 173–174
    quercifolia, 173
Fig trees, 163
  miniature creeping, 163, 173
Firefern, 169–170
Fish emulsion formulas, 105, 108
Fittonia verschaffeltii, 169
Fixtures for light gardens, 19–31
  circline tubes, 21
  designs, 24–25
  freestanding, 7, 10
  furniture incorporating light fixtures, 73
  glarefree lights, 28–29
  glass cabinets, 25–28
  incandescent floods and spots, 29–30
    outdoor fixtures, 30
  light gardens, 34–35
    strip fixtures, 34
  miniature 8-watt tubes, 20
  Phytarium, 25
  plant stands and tiered carts, 20, 22
  portable, 9–10
  reflectors, 19–20
    aluminum, 19
    baked enamel, 19–20
  self-standing light garden, 33
  strip fixtures, 34
  table fixtures, 20–21
  theatrical effects, 30–31
  tiered stands, 23, 41–45
  use of automatic timers, 6, 25, 27, 58, 75
  use of mirrors, 34, 38–39
  Wardian cases, 28
  waterproof trays, 20
  watts per square foot, 36
  wedged louvers of plastic, 28–29
  with controlled ventilation, light and
      humidity, 25–27
  with two 40-watt bulbs, 7–8
Flaming-swords, 228
Flora Cart (Tube Craft Co.), 20, 39–40
Floralite Co., 24
Flowering plants, 209–221
  bulbs, 217–221
  fertilizers for, 108
  lamp choice, 55
  lamp watts per square foot, 36
Fluorescent lighting
  broad-spectrum tubes, 50–51, 54
    combination with incandescent bulbs,
      52–53

Fluorescent lighting (*cont.*)
  color of light, 50
  condition of lamps, 59–60
  Cool White lamps, 4–5, 16
  Daylight lamps, 16, 49, 54, 56
  distance and intensity, 37–38
  energy emission in color bands of 40-watt
      lamps, 47
  fixtures. *See* Fixtures for light gardens
  Gro-Lux tubes (Sylvania), 5–6, 16
    standard violet-blue-toned, 16
  Gro-Lux, Wide-Spectrum, 16, 21, 43, 47,
      49–51
  guidelines for growing plants, 58–59
  horticultural lamps, 4–5, 46–49, 54
    broad spectrum, 50-51, 74
    combinations, 52–53
    economy of, 52
  for indoor plants, 3–4
  installing in sockets, 64
  light-hours and intensities, 68–75
    low-light requirements, 6
  listed life of 40-watt tubes, 30
  lumens, 55–56
  multipurpose lights, 6–7
  power problems, 62–63
  quality of light, 46–67
  replacing tubes, 59–60, 62
  rosy-hued lamps, 50
  spectrum, 16, 46–48
    artificial lights, 48
    blue and red rays for photosynthesis, 46–
      47
    broad-spectrum tubes, 50–51, 54
    red rays for growth, 46–47, 53
  standard, 54–55
  to supplement sunlight, 5–6, 9, 55
  survey of lamps, 49
  Sylvania's Gro-Lux, 5–6, 16
    Wide-Spectrum, 16, 21, 43, 47, 49–51
  Warm White, 5, 49–54
  watts per square foot, 36
Foliage damage, 240
  cleaning leaves, 240
  effect of water and fertilizer, 240
  humidity problems, 239–240
  spots, 240–241
  yellowing due to mineral deficiency, 244–245
Foliage plants, 11, 43, 53, 163–179
  containers and watering, 87
  effect of Gro-Lux lamps on, 5–6, 16
  ferns, 176–179
  fertilizers for, 108, 164
  to grow in water, 173–176
  healthy growth, 37
  illuminated by incandescent bulbs, 29
  lamp watts per square foot, 36

Foliage plants (*cont.*)
   large, 84
   light-hours and intensities, 35, 163–164
   reflector incandescents for, 163-164
   trailers, creepers and climbers, 173–176
Foot-candle measurements, 56, 58
   for measuring brightness, 56–57
Freed Orchids, Malibu, California, 131
Fungicides, 246–247
   systemic, 236, 244, 246
Fungus and rot problems, 240, 246–247

Gardenias, 70, 110, 244
Garner, W. W., 69-70
Gasteria, 200
   x *Aloe*, 200
      'Spotted Beauty', 200
   x *Gasterhaworthia*, 200
      'Royal Highness', 200
   verrucosa, 200
x *Gastrolea*, 200
   'Spotted Beauty', 200
General Electric Co., 29
   horticultural lamps, 30, 49
Geranium (*pelargonium*), 66, 71, 153, 158
   chemical dwarfing, 155–156
   dwarfs and miniatures, 156
   fragrant foliage, 158
   high-light requirements, 36–37, 62
   light and fertilizer, 154
   ornamental foliage, 156
   potting, 103, 153
   propagation, 154–155
   temperature for, 153–154
   See also Pelargonium
German-violets, 212
Germinating seeds, 234
Gesneria, 120
   cuneifolia, 120
      'Lemon Drop', 120
      quebradillas, 120
Gesneriads, 52, 71, 74, 84, 113–129
   containers for, 87
   culture basics, 115
   dwarf strains, 114
   fertilizers for, 107
   fibrous-rooted genera, 114, 127
   flourescent lamps for, 16, 117
   growth styles, 114–115
   light-hours and intensities, 35, 116–117
      even illumination for, 113–114
      lamp watts per square foot, 36
   list of, 117–127
   pests, 242
   potting soil, 103, 115–116
   rhizome-rooted genera, 115
   temperature requirements, 11, 114

Gesneriads (*cont.*)
   tuberous-rooted genera, 115
   watering methods, 96, 116
   See also African-violets
Gloxinia, 88, 113, 115, 125, 126
   See also Sinningia
Golden-barrel cactus, 205
Golding, Jack, 181
Goodyeara pubescens, 152
Grape-ivy (*Cissus*), 61, 173
Gravel, for moisture trays, 41
Gravelin, Ruth, 194
Green Garde (Encap Products Co.), 110, 246
Greenhouses, indoor, 4
Green plants
   influence of light on, 18
   phytochrome and, 48
   sunlight and photosynthesis, 12, 46–47
Gro-Lux lamps (Sylvania), 5–6, 16, 56
   brightness, 57
   incandescents and, 53
   red rays, 48
   standard violet-blue-toned, 16
   starting seeds, 234
   Wide Spectrum, 16, 21, 43, 47, 49–51
Growth chambers, 63–64
Growth patterns
   compact, 51
   influence of light, 18
   effect of changes in red and far-red light, 47–48
   factors influencing, 58, 69
   potted plants, 9
   semitropical species, 17–18
   variations when grown under different light
      sources, 49
GTE Sylvania Company
   Gro-Lux lamps, 5–6, 16, 56
   horticultural lamps, 49
   Wide Spectrum Gro-Lux lamps, 16, 21, 43,
      47, 49–51
Guzmania, 226–227
   lingulata, 226
   lingulata var. *cardinalis*, 226
   'Magnifica', 227
Gymnocalycium species, 206
Gynura aurantiaca, 95, 174

Habitats for plants, 12–13
Haemanthus
   katherine, 219
   multiflorus, 219
Haemaria discolor, 152
   See also Ludisia discolor
Haworthia, 194–195, 200–201
   fasciata, 198, 200–201
   papillosa, 195, 201

Haworthia (*cont.*)
  subfasciata, 201
Heat, effect on plants, 54–58
  from fixtures, 77–78
Hedera helix, ivies, 61, 174
  'Conglomerata', 174
  'Itsy Bitsy', 174
Herbs, 43, 159–162
  light-hours and intensities, 159–160
  list of, 159–162
H-frame light gardens, 41–45
  design and construction, 42–44
Hibiscus, 244
High-light requirement species, 51, 62
  lamp watts per square foot, 36–37
Hippeastrum. See Amaryllis
Holiday gift plants, 9–10
Hollenberg, Del, 128
Hoodia, 201
Horticultural lamps, 5, 48–49, 54
  broad-spectrum, 50–51, 74
  economy of, 52
  rosy-hued lamps, 50
Horticultural societies, 248–250
  publications, 249–250
Houseplants, fluorescent lamps for, 4
Hoya, 213
  bella, 213
  carnosa cultivars, 213
    'Crimson king', 213
    'Exotica', 213
  lacunosa, 213
Hubbell, H. L., Inc., 73
Humidifiers, 82
Humidity requirements, 10, 13, 41, 58–59, 80–81
  foliage problems, 239–240
  misting plants, 82
  moisture trays, 82, 97
Hyacinths, 221
Hybrids, 13
Hydrogel soil amendment, 98
Hypocyrta. See Nematanthus
Hypoestes sanguinolenta, 169
Hyponex, chemical fertilizer, 105, 108, 154

Impatiens, 70, 213–214
  'Blue Velvet', 214
  Cyclone hybrids, 214
  'Elfin', 214
  New Guinea, 70, 214
  'Scarlet Ripple', 55, 214
  'Star Fire', 214
Incandescent bulbs, 5
  broad-spectrum tubes and, 52–53
  combined with fluorescents, 29, 53
  efficiency of, 29
  floods and spots, 5, 29–30

Incandescent bulbs (*cont.*)
  heat problem, 54
  increasing bulb life, 53
  reflector lamps, 30
  sockets for, 40
  sodium lamps and, 64–65
Indoor Light Gardening Society, 181
Insecticides, use of, 241–244, 246
  combination treatments, 244
Intensity of light, 46
  frowth of plants and, 57
  guidelines for growing plants, 58–59
  placement of plants and, 56
  plants for various intensities, 61–62
  temperature and, 77
Iris, bulbous, 220
Iron chlorosis, 110
Iron deficiency, 110, 244–246
Isotox, 242, 243
Ivies, 54, 164
  English ivy, 174
  grape-ivies, 61, 173
  Kenilworth-ivy, 173
Ixora, 214
  coccinea, 214
  javanica, 214

Jadeplant, 199
Jasminum, 214
  gracile magnificum, 214
  nitidum, 214
  sambac 'Grand Duke', 214
Jelly beans, 203
Jesup, Phil, 150
Jewel box 'Crimson Glory' orchids, 142
Jiffy Mix, 99
Jones and Scully, 141
Jungle cacti, 194–195, 204, 206–208

Kalanchoe, 196, 201
  blossfeldiana, 70, 201
  daigremontiana, 202
  pinnata (syn. *Bryophyllum*), 201
  tomentosa (teddy-bear), 202
  tubiflora, 202
Karathane fungicide, 191, 247
Kartuz hybrids, 186
Kelthane insecticide, 242, 243
Kenilworth-ivy, 173
Koellikeria, 120
Kohleria, 115, 120–121
  'Connecticut Belle', 121
  digitaliflora, 121
  eriantha, 120–121
  'Longwood', 121
  'Princess', 121
Kys Mix (potting mix), 99

Lady-of-the-night orchid, 139
Ladyslipper orchids (*Paphiopedilum*), 15, 128, 146–148
Laelia orchids, 144–145
  pumilia, 144
  rubescens, 144
  Sophrolaelia Psyche, 145
Laeliocattleya hybrids, 142, 144
Laurus nobilis (bay leaf), 159–160
Leach, Dr. David G., 73
Leafmold, 101
Lepanthes orchids, 145
Lettuce, 64–65
Light color, fluorescent lamp, 50–53, 58
Light gardens
  benches and tables, 40
  bookcase gardens, 32–38
    construction, 32–34
    fixtures, 34–35
  cement treatment, 40–41
  constuction, 32–34
  custom-designed, 33–45
  distance and intensity, 38
  electric power requirements, 39, 62–63
    grounding plugs and sockets, 39–40
  fixtures, 34–35
  guidelines for, 58–59
  heat from enclosed gardens, 78
  H-frame, 41–45
  high-light requirements, 36–37
  increasing wattage, 37
  living art, 32
  louvers, 39
  mirrors, 38–39
  safety precautions, 39, 62–63
  size and type of lamps, 36
  tiered gardens, 41–45
Light-hour requirements, 68–75, 77
  biorhythms, 69
  dark spots, 68–69
  effects of temperature, 74–75
  photoperiod groups, 69–70
    indeterminate plants, 69, 71
    long night, 70
    short night, 70
  seedlings, 73–74
Light intensity, 12–13, 58
Light meters, 60–61
Light stands, 6–7
Lily-of-the-Nile, 209
Limestone, 100, 110
Lipstick Vines, 114–115
Livingston, Norman, 38
Loam, for potting mixes, 101
Logee's greenhouse, 186
Long-day (short-night) plants, 70, 73–74
Lord and Burnham Co., 26–27

Louvers, 39
  wedged, 28–29
Low-light requirement species, 15, 61
  foliage plants, 54–55
Low-pressure sodium (SOX) lamps, 64
Ludisia discolor, 152
Lumens, brightness of fluorescent tubes, 55–56
Lyon, Lyndone, 123

Madagascar jasmine-vine, 217
Maidenhair ferns, 178
Malathion, 242, 243, 244
Malpighia coccigera, 214
Mammillaria bocasana, 205
  elongata, 205
Maranta (orchids), 16, 167
  leuconeura kerchoveana, 170
Marble-vine, 203
Marigolds, 64–65
  hybrids, 71
Marjoram hortensis, 161
Marko Co., 29
Masdevallia, 145
Mealybug orchids (*ornithocephalus*), 146
Mealybugs, 242
Measuring light intensity, 58
  energy emission in color bands of 40 watt lamps, 47
  foot-candles, 56–57
  light meters for, 57–58, 60–61
  lumens, 55–56
  Spectral Energy Distribution (SED) curves, 58
  watts per square foot, 36, 57
Medium-light requirement species, 25, 61
  lamp watts per square foot, 36
  Sylvania's Gro-Lux for, 50
Melaleuca hypericifolia, 169, 245
Mentha cultivars (mint), 161
  citrata, 161
  rotundifolia, 161
Mericlones, 141, 142
Meristem propagation, 135, 137, 229
Mexican animalito pots, 94
Mexican foxglove, 210
Microclimates, 11, 13, 78–79
Mikkelsens Inc., 190
Mildew prevention, 191, 245, 246
Miltassia hybrid orchid, 145
Miltonia orchids, 145
  Bremen, 145
  clowesii, 145
  Goodale Moir, 145
  roezlii, 145
  spectabilis, 145
  vexillaria, 145
Mimosa pudica, 169
Mineral dificiencies, 108, 246

Mint (*Mentha* cultivars), 161
Miracle-Gro fertilizers, 105, 106, 108
Mirrors for light gardens, 34, 38-39
Mist for plants, 82
Mistletoe cactus, 208
Moisture trays, 41, 82, 97
Moses-in-the-boat, 215-216
Multipurpose lights, 6-7
Muscari bulbs, 220

Nakamotoara hybrid orchids, 145
Narcissus
   miniature, 88
   semihardy paperwhite, 221
Nasturtium, climbing, 217
Natur-Escent (Duro-Lite, Inc.), 51
Nematanthus, 121
   'Black Magic', 121
   'Cheerio', 121
   gregarius, 121
   wettsteinii, 121
Neofinetia falcata, orchids, 145
Neoregelia, 227
   carolinae tricolor, 227
Nephrolepsis, 178
   cordifolia 'Duffii', 178
   exaltata (Boston fern), 178, 238
   'Fluffy Ruffles', 178
Netherlands Bulb Institute, 220
Nicotiana tabacum, 18
Nicotine sulfate, 241
Nidularium, 227
   innocentii, 227
   lineatum, 227
Night-length (dark hours), 58, 69-70
   plant reactions to, 68-75
Nitrogen, nutrient for plants, 105
Notocactus species, 206

Ocimum basilicum (basil), 159
Odontocidium hybrid orchids, 146
Odontoglossum orchids, 13, 78, 145-146
   aspôglossium, 146
   colmanara, 146
   crispum hybrids, 146
   odontocidium, 146
Olive, fragrant, 169
Oncidium orchids, 146
   ampliatum, 146
   cheirophorum, 146
   Goldiana, 146
   Kalihi, 131
   ornithorhynchum, 146
Opuntia (cacti), 14
   microdasys, 205
Orchids, 9, 11, 38, 61, 70, 73-74, 75, 84, 128-152

Orchids (*cont.*)
   accelerating growth, 132
   cattleya-type, 62
   commercial control of blooming, 130-131
   containers for, 86-77, 88, 134
   culture basics, 132-137
   environmental conditions, 78-79
   epiphytic, 15-16, 96, 97, 99, 132-134
      potting, 109
   fertilizers, 107, 134
   fluorescent lamps for, 15
   foliage, 152
   humidity requirements, 134
   light-hour and intensities, 129-131
      high-light requirements, 13, 35, 36, 51, 128-129
      medium-light requirements, 128
   list of, 137-152
   moth orchids, 128-129
   need air circulation, 83
   night temperatures, 130
   orchid-cactus, 207
   potting mixes and fertilizers, 99-100, 134
   propagating, 135-137, 229
      meristem process, 135, 137
      sexual reproduction, 232-233
   pseudobulbs, 134
   seedlings, 131-132
   sunlight requirements, 14-16
   terrestrials, 133
   watering methods, 96-97, 134
Orchids, The: A Scientific Survey (Withner), 132
Origanum vulgare (oregano), 161
Ornamentals Research Laboratory, Beltsville, Maryland, 64
Ornithocephalus orchids, 146
   bicornis, 146
   grandiflorus, 146
Ortho Flotox (fungicide), 247
Osmanthus fragrans, 169
   ilicifolius variegatus, 169
Osmocote fertilizer, 107, 108
Oxalis
   hedysaroides rubra, 169-170
   martiana 'Aureo-reticulata', 170-171
   regnelli, 215

Pachyphytum, 202
Palms, 37, 163-164
Pansy orchids, 145
Paphiopedilum (ladyslipper orchids), 15, 61, 100, 133, 146-148
   bellatulum, 148
   ciliolare, 147
   concolor, 147, 148
   glaucophyllum, 148

Paphiopedilum (cont.)
  insigne, 148
  Maudiae, 147
  niveum, 148
  sukhakulii, 149
  venustum, 149
Paracube louvers, 28-29, 39
Paramount hybrids, 206
  'Pink and White', 205
Para-Wedge louvers, 28-29
Park Seed Co., 24, 235
Parodia aureispina, 206
Parsley (Petroselinum hortense), 161-162
Peanut-cactus, 204
Peatmoss, 101
Pelargonium, 153-158
  'Apple Blossom Rosebud', 155
  Carefree strain, 154, 156
  domesticum hybrids, 154, 156
  dwarfs and miniatures, 156
    'Acturus', 156
    'Alpha', 156
    'Artic Star', 156
    fragrant foliage, 156
      crispum 'Prince Rupert variegated', 158
      graveolens 'Little Gem's', 157, 158
      radens 'Dr. Livingston', 157, 158
      x scarboroviae 'Countess of Scarborough',
        157-158
  hortorum hybrids, 154
  Martha Washington hybrids, 154
  'Mrs. Henry Cox', 156
  See also Geraniums
Pellionia
  daveauana, 174
  pulchra, 174-175
Peperomia, 163, 171
  'Little Fantasy', 49
  obtusifolia, 231
  sandersii, 171, 231
Periodicals, list of, 250
Perlite (volcanic rock), 6, 21, 101
  for moisture trays, 41
Persian-shield, 173
Persian-violet (Exacum affine), 70
Pests or diseases, 239-247
  combination treatments, 244
  insecticides for, 241-242
  list of common pests, 242-244
  treatment for, 241-244
Peters African-violet fertilizer, 108
Peters water-soluable fertilizers, 104, 106, 108
Petroselinum hortense (parsley), 161
  carnum, 161
  'Paramount', 162
Phalaenopsis (moth orchids), 70, 88, 128-129,
  132, 136, 149

Phalaenopsis (cont.)
  amabilis, 129-130
  dendrobium, 130, 142-143
  hybrids, 149
  lueddemanniana, 149
  schilleriana, 130
  violacea, 149
Philodendron, 15, 54, 71, 163-164, 172, 174
  low-light requirements, 6, 61
  'Lynette', 172
  oxycardium, 163
  wendlandii, 172
Phosphorus, 105
Photographic light meter, 60-61
Photoperiods, 70-71
Photosynthesis, 12, 46-48
Physan (formally called Consan), 247
Phytarium cabinet for plants, 25
Phytochrome, 48
Phyto-Gro chamber, 25-26
Pilea, 176
  involucrata, 176
  'Norfolk', 175
  repens, 173, 176
Pineapple, 222, 225
Pineapple-lily, 219
Placement of plants, intensity of light and, 56
Plant breeders, 13
Plant-Gro lamp (Westinghouse), 50
Plant-Gro fluorescents, incandescents, 53
Plant Lite incandescent bulbs, 29
Plantariums, solar, 26-27
Plants and growing supplies, list of sources,
  251-258
Plastic bags, to keep plants moist, 84
Plastic pots, 85-86, 88
  self-watering containers, 89-90
  square pots, 86
Plastic tent, to control humidity, 81, 84
Platycerium (ferns), 179
Plectranthus coleioides marginatus
  minima, 171
Pleurothallis orchids, 145, 149-150
  lanceola, 150
Plexiglas shelves, 67
Poinsettias, 70
  Christmas, 200
Polkadot plant, 169
Polypodium aureum (ferns), 238
Polyscias, 172
  fruticosa elegans, 172
  guilfoylei victoriae, 172
Polystachya orchids, 150
  luteola, 150
  phalax, 150
Polystichum tsus-simense, 179
Pomegranate, dwarf, 215

Poracel, slow-release fertilizer, 107
Portability of plants, 9
Portulaca, 202
  'Tuffet', 202
Portulacaria, 202
  afra-variegata, 202
Potassium (potash), 105
Pothos (Devil's Ivy), 61, 163
Pots. *See* Containers
Potting mixes, 99–103
  acid-alkaline balance, 110
  basic soil mixture, 99, 102–103
  cacti and succulents, 196
  fertilizers, 103–110
  ingredients, 100–102
    bark chips, 100
    dolomite limestone powder, 100
    leafmold, 101
    loam, 101
    peatmoss, 101
    perlite, 101
    sand, 101
    sphagnum moss, 102
    vermiculite, 102
  pasteurized, 239
  for seeds, 237
  soil additives, 100
  soilfree mixes, 99
Powdery mildew, 246
Precise (slow-release fertilizer), 107, 108
Primula malacoides (primrose), 74–75
Propagation, 229–238
  asexual, 229–231
    bulblets, 229
    clump divisions, 229, 231, 238
    leaf cuttings, 229, 231, 236
    offsets, 229
    stems, 229
    tip cuttings, 229, 230, 236
  creating hybrids, 232
  cross-pollinated seedlings, 232
  damp-off protection, 236
  ferns, 238
  hybrids from seed, 233
  lamps for, 234
  orchids, 135, 137
    meristem process, 135–137, 229
  procedures, 235–236
  seed funds of tropical plant societies, 233
  seedlings, 232
  seed sowing, 237–238
  self-cross, 232
  sexual reproduction, 232–233
  special seed, 233
  temperature for, 76–77, 234–235
  vegetative, 229, 235–236
Pseudoripsalis macrantha, 208

Pteris species, 238
  multifida, 178
Punica granatum nana, 215
Purple-heart vine, 176
Pyrethrum, 241

Quality of light, 46–67
  lumens, 55–56
  reflective values, 65–67
Queens-tears, 225

Rattlesnake-plantain, 152
Rebutia species of cactus, 206
Rechsteineria, 115
  See also Sinningia
Red spider mites, 243
Redwood planters, 87
Reflector fixtures, 19–20
  incandescent bulbs, 29–30
  value of, 65–67
Renanthopsis orchids, 149
Repotting plants, 104
  See also Potting mixes
Research studies, 64
Rhipsalis
  mesembryanthemoides, 208
  quellenbambensis, 208
Rhododendron seedlings, 73
Rhoeo spathacea (syn *R. discolor*), 215–216
Rieger, Otto, 189
Rieger begonia cultivars, 107, 189–190, 246
Rivina humilis (rouge-plant), 50
Rodricidium hybrid orchids, 151
Rodriguezia orchids, 150–151
  granadensis, 151
  secunda, 151
  venusta, 151
Room dividers, 7
  H-frame light garden, 41–45
Rooting leaves, light requirements, 36–37
Rootone powder, 135, 234
Roots
  maintaining healthy, 239
  pruning, 96
  root rot, 246
  techniques for healthy roots, 97
Roscoflex reflection media (Rosco Labs), 34, 67
Rosemary (*Rosmarinus officianalis*), 162
Roses, 216
  miniature, 71, 216, 246
  'Willie Mae', 216
Rosmarinus officianalis (rosemary), 162
Rosy-hued lamps, 50
Ruellia makoyana, 172

Safety precautions, 39
Sage (*Salvia officianalis*), 162
Saintpaulia hybrids, 113–114, 121–123
  See also African-violets
Sakrette (sand), 101
Salvia officianalis (sage), 162
  rutilans, 162
Sand, in potting mixes, 101
Sansevieria, 195, 203
  chrenbergii, 193
  hanii, 231
  trifasciata hahnii, 203
Sarcohilus falcatus orchids, 151
Saville, Harm, 216
Saxifraga stolonifera (strawberry-geranium),
    70, 172
  sarmentosa, 172
  'Tricolor', 172
Saylor, William, 121
Scales on houseplants, 243
Schefflera actionophylla (*Brassaia*), 172
Schlumbergera (Christmas cacti), 75, 206–
    208
Scientific name of plant, use in ordering
    plants, 252
Seaweed fertilizers, 106
Sedum, 203
  morganianum, 203
  multiceps, 203
  pachyphyllum, 203
  rubrotinctum, 91
Seed funds of tropical plant societies, 233
Seedlings
  chemical dwarfing, 155–156
  containers and watering, 87
  damp-off protection, 236, 246
  fungus problems, 246
  high-light requirements, 36–37, 73
  long-day benefits, 73–74
  Sylvania's Gro-Lux, 50
Seemannia latifolia, 123
Selaginella, 61
  uncinata, 164
Semitropical species, 17
Senecio, 203
  herreianus, 203
  macroglossus, 203
Setcreasea purpurea, 176
Shell No-Pest strips, 244
Shoplite Company, 20, 22, 24
Showering plants, 240
Shrimp-plant, 210
Sinningia, 113–114, 123–126
  'Bright Eyes', 115, 125, 126
  cardinalis, 126
  'Cindy Ella', 124, 125
  concinna, 125

Sinningia (*cont.*)
  'Dollbaby', 115, 124
  eumorpha, 126
  hybrids, 113–114
    speciosa, 115
  'Laurie', 126
  leucotricha (Brazilian edelweiss), 126
  'Melinda', 126
  miniature, 124–125, 126
  pusilla, 125
  regina, 126
  'Robin Hood', 125
Smithiantha, 115, 126–127
  'Little Tudor', 127
  'Little Wonder', 127
  'Temple bells', 115, 127
Snails and slugs, 243–244
Sochrensia bruchii (syn. *Lobivia*), 197
Societies and periodicals, list of, 250
Sodium lamps, 64–65
Soils
  acid-alkaline balance, 110
  moisture, 13
  pasteurized potting, 239
  potting mixes and fertilizers, 99–110
Solar Plantariums, 26–27
Sophrolaelia Psyche hybrid orchid, 145
Sophronitis orchids, 141
  cernua, 151
  coccinea, 151
  grandiflora, 151
SOX lamps, 64–65
Spanish moss, 222, 228
Spathiphyllum, 61, 164, 217
  clevelandii (syn. *patinii*), 217
  'Mauna Loa', 217
Spectral Energy Distribution (SED) curves,
    58
Spectrum, 46
  artificial lights, 48
  blue and red rays for photosynthesis, 46–47
  broad-spectrum tubes, 50–51
  effect of blue and red rays on growth, 46–
    48, 53
Sphagnum moss, 102
Spider-aralia, 169
Spider orchids, 139
Spider plants (*Chlorophytum comosum*),
    167–168
Springtails, 244
Squills, 88
Stanhopea orchids, 151
  eburnea, 151
  oculata, 151
Stapelia, 194, 203
  gigantea, 203
  hirsuta, 203

Stapelia (*cont.*)
  semota lutea, 203
  variegata, 203
Stelis orchids, 152
Stem rot, 246
Stephanotis floribunda, 217
Stern's Miracid, 110
Stern's Miracle-Gro, 105, 106, 108
Stewart, Fred A., Co., 141
Stawberry-begonia, 172
Strawberry-geranium, 70, 172
Streptocarpus (cape-primrose), 115, 127
  'Constant Nymph', 127
  hybrids, 127
  'Maasens White', 127
  'Mini Nymph', 127
  'Ultra Nymph', 127
Strobilanthes dyerianus, 173
Styrofoam pots, 87
Succulents, 84, 193-208
  cacti, 204-208
    desert cacti, 204-206
    jungle cacti, 204, 206-208
  containers for, 87, 88-89
  fluorescent lamps for, 195
  light hours and intensities, 194-196
    high-light requirements, 35, 36, 51
  list of, 198-202
  pests, 242
  soil, pots and fertilizers, 196
  sunlight *vs.* fluorescents, 193-194
  use of insecticides, 242
  See also Cacti
Sudbury soil testing kits, 110
Summer-blooming species, 70
Sunlight
  brightness, 12-14
  day-length responses, 18
  fluorescent lights to supplement, 5-6, 9, 55
  growth changes and variations in, 17-18
  in nature, 12-18
  source of energy, 12
  sun and shade, 14-15
  supplemental light, 55
  variations in color, 15-16
Supplemental light, 5-6, 9, 55
Sure-Fire Potting Mix, 99
Sylvania fluorescent tubes
  Cool Lux bulb, 30
  Gro-Lamp, 20
  Gro-Lux fluorescent tubes, 5-6, 16, 56-57
  Wide Spectrum Gro-Lux, 16, 21, 43, 47, 49-51
Syngonium, 164, 176
  podophyllum cultivars, 164, 176

Tall plants
  overhead lights for, 29, 33
  watering, 33

Temperature requirements, 10-11, 13, 58, 76-77
  effects of, 74-75
  electric heat cables, 80
  light and, 77
  microclimates, 11, 78-79
  for propagation, 234-235
Terrariums, 92-93
  enclosed bookshelf light gardens, 34-35
  gesneriads for, 115
  miniature 8-watt tubes, 20
  orchids, 152
  partridge-berry, 152
  watering, 93
Thanksgiving cactus, 206-207
Thermometers, maximum-minimum, 79-90
3-M Precise slow-release fertilzer, 107, 108
Thymus vulgaris (thyme), 162
  'Caprilands', 162
  'Golden Lemon', 162
  serpyllum, 162
Tiered gardens, 41-45
Tiger-jaws, 200
Tillandsia, 223, 227-228
  cyanea, 227
  ionantha, 228
  lindenii, 227
  usneoides (Spanish moss), 222, 224, 228
Timber Toppers (spring-loaded), 41
Tobacco studies, 18
Tomatoes, 64-65
  seedlings, 71
Trademarks and patents, 190
Tradescantia, 176
  albiflora, 176
  blossfeldiana, 176
  fluminensis variegata, 177
  sillamontana, 176
  velutina, 177
Trailers, creepers, and climbers, 173-176
Trays for pots, 41
  filled with moist gravel or perlite, 41
  moisture, 82, 97
Tropacolum tricolor, 217
Tropical plants, under lights, 9
Tropical regions, sun and shade, 14-15
Tube Craft Company, 20, 24
  watering aids, 98
Tuberous plants, 217-218
Tufflite pots, 87
Tulips, 221

Ultraviolet rays, 12
Union Carbide Corporation, 98
United States Department of Agriculture
  permits to bring in foreign plants, 251
  research studies, 18, 64

Vacation time, care of plants, 83-84
Vanda orchids, 137, 145

274

Vapona-impregnated strips, 244
Vazquez, Amado, 132
Veltheimia, 219–220
  glauca (syn. *capensis*), 219–220
  'Rosabla', 220
  viridiflora, 220
Velvet-passion-vine, 174
Verilux TruBloom (Verilux Co.), 51, 55, 56
Vermiculite, 102
Vines, 173–176
Vita-Lite (Duro-Lite, Inc.), 21, 49, 51, 55
  Power-Twist version, 21
Viterra, hydrogel soil amendment, 98
Vriesea, 223, 228
  splendens, 228

Wandering Jew, 176
  striped, 176
Warm-White lamps, 49, 54
  for propagations, 234
Watering methods, 93–98
  bottom-watering, 94–96
  during vacation period, 83–84
  fertilizer salts, 96
  guide to watering, 93–94
  hydrogel soil amendment, 98
  light gardens, 94–96
  self-watering containers, 89–90

Watering methods (*cont.*)
  standard top-watering, 96–97
  terrariums, 93
  watering aids, 98
Watts per square foot, 36, 57
Westinghouse horticultural lamps, 49–50
  Agro-Lite, 50, 234
  Plant-Gro lamp, 50
Whiteflies, 244, 245
Wide-Spectrum Gro-Lux, 16, 21, 43, 47, 49–50, 51–52, 54
  brightness, 57
Wilson, Helen Van Pelt, 123
Winter-flowering plants, 70
Withner, Dr. Carl, 132
Wood, treatment to preserve, 40

Yellow foliage and iron deficiency, 244–246

Zadescantia, 220
  elliottina, 220
  rehmannii, 220
Zebra haworthia, 201
Zebra plant (*Aphelandra squarrosa*), 70, 210
Zebrina, 5, 7, 176
  creeping, 5
Zygocactus (Thanksgiving cactus), 208
  trunculus delicutus, 208